THE PARTY TIME GAME BOOK

Compiled
by Naoma Clark

WORD BOOKS
WACO, TEXAS

CONTENTS

PART ONE

•
•
•

DON'T JUST STAND THERE

If the group is large and many of the guests strangers to one another, a party may "feel stiff" and formal as it first begins. With carefully planned activities during these initial moments, the host can soon arrange to have everyone pleasantly acquainted as well as establish a good feeling of fun. The sooner guests are able to relax and feel comfortable with one another, the better chances are they will enjoy each other's company for the evening. The games included in this section are designed to introduce guests quickly and move the party off to a good start.

1. MUSICAL MIXER

As each guest arrives, he is given the name of a well-known song on a slip of paper. Be sure several people have been given the same song. Guests are instructed to begin searching for others holding the name of the song they have. When groups have collected, give everyone a few minutes to become acquainted and then call on each "ensemble" to perform.

2. YOUR NAME OR YOUR ADDRESS

Place two boxes near the entrance. One contains slips of paper with the names of the guests expected at the party. The other contains their addresses. As each guest arrives, pin one slip from both boxes on his clothing. Instruct participants to move around the room in an effort to locate guests wearing their particular name or address. They must ask the guests contacted whether or not the name and address pinned on them belongs to the other. If it does, they trade until finally everyone in the room has located his own name and address and is wearing it pinned to his lapel.

3. PORTRAIT ARTISTS

Give each guest a large sheet of paper and a pencil. He must write his full name on one side of the paper and then hand it back to be redistributed. Instruct "artists" to draw the portrait of the guest whose name is written on the paper they now have. When completed, portraits are put on display with each player attempting to locate his own.

4. ADVERTISING SPECIALISTS

Before the party, tape up magazine ads around the room, being careful to cut out any writing which might identify the product advertised. As each guest arrives, he is given a paper and pencil and told to attempt an identification of as many products by brand name being advertised as possible before he sits down.

5. SWEET OR SOUR

Guests are divided into two teams and lined up facing each other just a few feet apart. One team is called "heads" and the other "tails." The game leader tosses a coin and calls out the side that turns up. If it comes up heads, the team so named must laugh and smile while the tails team attempts to keep sober faces. The heads may try to make the tails laugh. All who laugh on the sober side must join the opposite team as the coin is tossed again.

6. INSTANT WORDS

As each guest arrives, pin a card with a large alphabetical letter printed on it to one sleeve. At a given signal, guests are to join into groups to compose four letter words. Members of the first "word" to greet the hostess receive a prize.

7. Autograph Hounds

At a gathering where people do not know one another well, give each guest a large autograph card as he
arrives, with instructions to secure the signature and address of each person he talks to. A prize may be awarded
later for the longest list of autographs.

8. Hooting Handkerchief

This party opener is effective for creating a happy party
mood. Although the laughing may be forced at the start,
it soon becomes quite spontaneous and natural .

A leader stands where everyone can easily see him. He
tosses a handkerchief into the air. As long as it is floating
down, everyone laughs hilariously. As soon as it touches
the floor, however, all players must stop laughing and assume a very serious expression. Those who laugh when the
handkerchief is not in the air are eliminated and must
stand to one side where they are allowed to assist in attempts to make those players still in competition laugh out
of turn. Players who do not laugh when the handkerchief
is in the air must also be eliminated. The distance the
handkerchief is thrown up should be varied to confuse
players as to the length of time they should laugh.

9. Introductions

Here is a good mixer to help everyone at the party become familiar with the names of the other guests. After
everyone is seated, the leader stands and says, "I'm glad to

meet you. My name is Mr. Martin." The next person stands and says, "How do you do, Mr. Martin, my name is Miss Simpson." The third in line stands and says, "How do you do, Mr. Martin and Miss Simpson, my name is Mr. Roberts." The fourth repeats the guests names already given and then adds his own. The game continues until everyone has been mentioned with each guest listing the names of those who have already introduced themselves. If a player has difficulty, he may be prompted by other guests rather than eliminated.

10. HA, HA, HA

Players are seated in a circle. The first player begins by saying, "Ha." The second in turn says, "Ha, Ha." The third adds, "Ha, Ha, Ha," the fourth, "Ha, Ha, Ha, Ha," and this continues around the circle with each guest adding one more "Ha." The "Ha's" must be uttered without laughing. This soon proves difficult and will start the entire circle chuckling. Players laughing without managing to get out all their "Ha, Ha's" are eliminated, until one lone sober face emerges as champion.

11. LUCKY SPOT

Announce early that there is a lucky spot designated in the room, and sometime during the party a signal will be given. The guest standing or sitting nearest this spot will win a special prize. It might be wise to postpone giving the signal (this should be done with a great deal of fanfare) until late in the party in order to maintain interest.

12. Reporter

As guests arrive, give each a news story previously clipped from the newspaper. Tell them to read it and then pin it to their clothing. Guests then circulate about the room asking each person for a run down on news stories pinned to them. Allow sufficient time for reporters to snoop out the scoops before collecting the clippings again. Guests are given a pencil and paper to write down highlights from as many stories as possible, numbering each.

13. Famous Characters

Before the party, prepare slips on which you have written the names of famous people, both present day and historical characters. As the guests arrive, pin a slip on the back of each without letting him know what it says. Guests read one another's name and then carry on a conversation as if talking to the person whose name is written on the paper. As this continues, each guest attempts to guess which famous person he is supposed to be.

14. Find Your Proverb

Write a different well-known proverb on a number of plain cards and then cut the cards exactly in half. Hide half of the cut proverbs around the room and give half a proverb card to each guest. At the go signal, players begin searching for the missing half to their card.

15. Travel Music

When all the guests have arrived, gather them in the

living room and number them off in pairs. Each couple is told to wander around the room while a record is being played. As they walk together, they begin to become acquainted. When the music stops, the game leader calls out, "travel in threes." Immediately everyone attempts to find two players to form a threesome. Music starts again and the units of three wander around in time to music while everyone introduces himself to the others in his group. Once again the music stops and the leader calls out, "travel in fours." This time there is a rush to make up groups of four. Any player unable to join a group must wait until a new unit is named. This may continue as long as desired, with as many break ups as necessary to shuffle the guests around and get them acquainted.

16. PASS THE SMILE

Guests are seated in a circle with someone "it" in the center. Everyone in the circle must keep a straight face until "it" stands in front of him. That player must immediately smile, but not laugh. "It" then says, "Wipe that silly smile off your face and pass it along." The grinning player wipes his hand across his mouth and the smile must be completely gone. If he fails to get rid of his smile, or laughs in the process, he changes places with "it" and must repeat the procedure with another player in the circle. However, if he is successful in passing his smile, the player receiving it smiles while it goes to him and repeats the ritual.

17. MYSTERY LAP

Seat guests in a circle with someone blindfolded in the

center. Have players move around so their location is not
known to the blindfolded person. That player, assisted by
other guests to prevent accidents, moves to someone's chair
and sits down in his lap. He says, "Howdy," and the person selected must disguise his voice to answer, "Howdy."
The blindfolded player then asks, "What is your name?"
The player answers, "That's your guess." If the blindfolded
player guesses correctly, they change places. If not, "it"
tries another lap.

18. Laughing Machine

Everyone stands in a circle with the "laughing machine"
situated in the center. When the leader raises his arms, he
starts the "machine" and players must respond by laughing
as hard as they can. As soon as the leader begins to lower
his arms, however, the laughter must die down until by the
time his arms are at his sides, the circle is completely silent. Anyone letting out even a small snicker must act as
the laughing machine for the next round. If more than one
player laughs, have several "machines" operating in the
center.

19. Who is Missing?

If there is a large enough group at the party, this "mixer"
can provide a lot of fun. When everyone has been introduced so the first name of each guest is familiar, seat
players in a circle with someone chosen as "it" standing
blindfolded in the center. Guests move from chair to chair
in the circle. One of the seated players leaves the room.

"It" then removes his blind and tries to guess which person is missing. If he cannot, that person returns to the game and "it" is again blindfolded for another try. If he is successful, the person who left the room is "it."

20. SPECIAL SIGNATURE

Give each player a sheet of paper and a pencil. Down the left hand border of the sheet, write the letters of a word associated with the theme of the party such as Halloween, Christmas, Birthday, Wedding, etc. When the signal is given, players mill about gathering signatures of guests whose first, last or middle name begins with one of the letters in the word lettered out. Players ask those guests to sign their name opposite the appropriate letter. At the end of a time limit, the player with the most signatures is awarded a prize.

21. KEEP A STRAIGHT FACE

Guests are seated in a circle, with the game leader initiating the action. He takes his left hand and touches some part of the face of the guest seated on his left. He keeps a finger glued to this spot while the person on his left touches a spot on the face of the person on his left. This continues around the circle. Anyone laughing must leave the game.

Play continues, with the leader initiating a different action each time. He might touch a nose, pull on his neighbor's hair, pinch an ear, etc. When a player leaves because he has laughed, the circle may be gathered closer by mov-

ing chairs together without any players losing contact.
Have eliminated players take their chairs out with them.

22. TALKING CONTEST

This mixer can be effectively used with younger children, especially if some of them are quite shy. Two contestants face one another and are given a subject. Both
must continue talking on this subject as loudly and rapidly
as possible for 30 seconds.

PART TWO

●
●
●

THE SKY IS THE LIMIT

The games listed in this section are appropriate for group adult play outdoors. Whether the occasion is a picnic, lawn party, retreat, or informal get together in the backyard, program a good selection of outdoor games, and the sky is the limit to the fun that can be had.

23. Roman Chariot Race

Players are divided into teams of six or eight players. One "driver" is chosen from each team and the other members act as his "horses." Give the team a rope. Horses join hands to hitch themselves together, and the horse on each side holds either end of the rope which represents the lines the driver uses to guide his team. Line up teams at a starting point and, if possible, use a toy cap pistol to signal go. Chariots race over a course previously laid out for them. Horses may not break loose from their position, and the driver must keep his hands on the lines at all times during the race. Any group breaking these rules is disqualified.

24. Dribble Keep Away

Have players choose sides to form two teams, and designate one team to begin. Rules of the game dictate that any player having possession of a basketball must dribble it at least ten times before he can pass it to a team mate. Members of the opposing team try to dribble the ball out of his hands. Watch closely for fouls; when one is committed, the team fouled takes the ball out of bounds.

25. Batty Baseball Game

Arrange the ball diamond in the same way as for a regular softball game, except keep the distance between bases not more than half of a regulation diamond. Fielders are equipped with bushel baskets or large sacks. Batters stand with their backs to the pitcher and must bat with a backward motion. Also, when the ball is hit, the batter must run to first base backward. A ball may not be fielded by hand, but must be caught in a basket and thrown by swinging the container.

26. GOOFY RELAY

Divide contestants into two or more teams and have each team count off consecutively. Designate a special method of racing for each number counted. As the race gets underway, identically numbered runners from each team race to the opposite goal line and back. The first contestant may be assigned to hop on one foot. The second may have to jump backwards. The third may have to skip sideways, etc.

27. TWO HEADED RACE

Staple a series of two paper sacks together at the bottoms. When time for the race, divide contestants into pairs and give them the two-headed hats to put on. With their heads thus joined, they run toward a goal line, holding both hand on their heads to keep the hat in place. If the hat falls off, it must be put back before contestants may continue racing.

28. ONE-LEGGED TUG OF WAR

Line up teams on opposite ends of a strong rope and

stage a tug of war with contestants staying on one foot
at all times. Right and left feet may be used, one at a time.
Keep a referee or two on hand to eliminate rule breakers.

29. ROPE SKIPPING RACE

Give each contestant a rope to jump and start them
racing—skipping rope—toward a goal line. This race is
especially amusing when there are men and boys par-
ticipating.

30. THREE-LEGGED RACE

Contestants line up at a starting point. Each runner
chooses a partner, who stands beside him with the right
leg and foot of one contestant held tightly against the
left leg and foot of his partner. Tie their legs together and
have teams race three-legged following a brief practice
session.

31. CREATION IN STONE

Divide the group into teams of four or more each, and
mark off an area in the dirt for each team. If it is permissible
to do so, supply a large pile of stones to be used by team
"artists" in creating an interesting display, lining up rows
of stones to outline a scene, message, etc.

32. WHEELBARROW RACE

This is a favorite picnic contest for men and boys. Racers

choose partners, with one person assuming a wheelbarrel position. He does this by keeping his body stiff, face down, walking on both hands while his partner holds up his feet behind him. Contestants race to a line twenty or thirty feet distant, reverse positions, and race back to the starting line.

33. SAHARA WHISTLING CONTEST

Here is another picnic favorite. Give each participant three soda crackers. At the signal to go, each contestant jams all the crackers into his mouth an once. The first to be able to whistle after eating the crackers is declared the winner.

This contest can work on a team basis. Give each member three crackers and have the first contestant on each team eat his share. As soon as he can whistle, the next team member in line downs his crackers and whistles. The first team finishing wins.

34. ROCKET LAUNCH

Give each contestant a large balloon. All balloons should be uniform, both in size and shape. Each player blows up his balloon as far as he dares, then holds it in the air by pinching the head. Contestants take turns stepping up to the "launching pad" to let their balloon rockets blast off. The balloon traveling the farthest distance from the pad wins.

To score accurately, you might have players stand on the exact spot where their deflated balloon landed.

When a balloon orbits farther than any other, the contestant standing closer to the launch pad is eliminated so that, finally, the person farthest out in space is declared champion astronaut.

35. BALANCE PILLOW FIGHT

Here is a contest certain to generate a lot of laughter and good fun. Place two barrels, small baskets, or boxes of equal proportion about three feet apart. Place a contestant on each barrel and give him a pillow. At the signal to start, the blows get underway. The first contestant to force his opponent to lose his balance is the winner.

36. IT'S ALIVE

This is an appropriate game to play around an evening campfire. Players sit or stand in a circle. A lighted match is given to the person beginning the game. He hands it, still lighted, to the person on his right, saying, "It's alive." The person taking it passes the lighted match along to the person on his right, making the same statement.

Play continues until the match goes out before the person holding it can pass it on. This might happen because it has burned so low it can no longer be held, or it might blow out. When this happens, the participant holds out the match to the person on his right and says, "It's alive." If the person accepts it anyway, he is eliminated from the game. However, if he refuses the match saying, "It's dead," the person still holding it is eliminated.

37. Don't Tread on Me

Mark off a circular playing area about six feet in diameter. Two contestants remove their shoes and step into this arena where, at the signal to begin, they try to step on each other's toes. No hands may be used. Contestants attempt to step on one another's toes while, at the same time, keeping the opponent off their own. The first to manage this is the winner.

38. Human Arrows

Drive several stakes into the ground, each about three feet apart. The space between the two center stakes is labeled the bull's eye and is given the highest point value. Less points are awarded for each area from the center out. The space outside either end of the target takes minus points from the score.

Depending on how many people are available, choose two or more players to act as archers. Then blindfold the human "arrows" for the archers to "shoot."

Proceed with the game by lining up the "arrows" together in front of the archers about thirty feet from the target area. One at a time, the archer aims his human arrow at the bull's eye and pushes him on his way. The arrow tries to walk forward as straight as possible in the direction he was pointed. As he nears the target, his archer calls out warnings so he will not trip over the stakes. The point at which he passes through the target decides the points earned for the archer.

39. Back to Back Tug of War

Stand two contestants back to back, with their arms linked at the elbows. Mark off two lines about ten feet in front of each contestant. When the signal is given, each contestant tries to drag, carry, or in some other way force his opponent to cross the line he faces.

40. Chinese Basketball

This game is played with the same rules as regular basketball, except that to score a point the ball must be thrown by a player through the hoop from underneath instead of through the top. Therefore, shots can only be scored right under the basket.

This is a good game to play on a small court or under a shooting basket.

41. Pie Eating Contest

Stand contestants in front of a table and place a piece of pie in front of each. Tie the pie eater's hands behind them and instruct the group that they must eat the pie "no hands." The first contestant to finish is the winner. Be sure to have someone on hand taking pictures!

42. Hats Off

Select two contestants and place a hat on each. Use

small hats that will perch lightly on top of the players' head. The point of the contest is for each to attempt to knock the hat off the other contestant's head, while at the same time keeping his own in position. Holding the hat on with either hand is not permitted.

43. HUMAN CROQUET

Set out a croquet course, using two people to form each arch with arms extended and hands clasped. Use blind-folded players as the balls. Each player has one "ball." Instead of hitting it, however, he turns the "ball" 'in the direction he must go and tells him how many steps to take. Beyond that, he is not allowed to do anything to guide his "ball" toward the arch.

Since the "ball" is blindfolded, he is quite likely to miss the arch as play progresses. Caution the blindfolded "balls" to keep their hands extended as they move forward in order to avoid injury. Verbal instruction may not be given, after a "ball" begins to move.

44. DONKEY

Here is a good game to play when you have only one basket available, but of course it can be easily played on any basketball court. There is no limit to the number who can play, but as interest in the activity might lag, it is best to keep the number of players down to six or eight.

Players number off, and this designates the order in which they will shoot during the contest. First, the leadoff man makes a shot. If he gets a basket, then number two must shoot from the exact position and in the same manner. If he makes a basket, too, then the next player repeats the successful shot.

However, if number two misses, he has a "D" against his name. The next time he misses, he picks up an "O". This continues until the word Donkey has been spelled out and the player is eliminated from the game.

The game is made more interesting as players try unusual shots, in an attempt to stump the next player in line.

45. TOE RELAY

Guests are divided into two or more teams for this unusual relay. Place half of each team on one goal and the remaining half on the other. Contestants remove their shoes and socks and place a pencil between the big toe and second toe of one foot.

At the signal to go, each contestant hops—he must not run or walk—across to the opposite goal line. If he drops the pencil, he must stop to put it back in position, using only his feet, before he can continue to the goal. When he reaches it, he holds out his foot for the next runner to pick up the pencil, and the relay continues.

46. SPLINTS

Tie a broomstick, or similar piece of wood, securely to each leg of the contestants in this race, preventing them from bending either knee. Then tie them up and proceed with typical racing activities.

47. HURDLE RACE

Divide players into two or more teams, at least eight members on each team. Line up the teams two abreast; with each contestant about an arm's length from his partner.

Give the first two members of each team a broomstick to hold between them. These two run down the length of their team, one on either side of the line, holding the broom near the ground for the team members to jump over. As soon as they reach the back, one of them races to the front of the line to hand the broomstick to the next pair. This continues until each pair has taken a turn carrying the "hurdle" from one end of its team line to the other.

48. SACK RACE

This picnic favorite dates back to grandfather's day. Each runner is given a large burlap bag to climb into, holding the edges of the sack with both hands as he runs and jumps across the race course to a goal line.

49. HANDICAPPED FOOTBALL

Tie the feet of each player with equal lengths of rope so that he can only take short steps. Form two teams and proceed with a typical game of football, keeping play restricted to a small area. This will provide lots of fun and requires real agility on the part of players.

50. STRETCHER BEARERS

Divide contestants into teams with five on a team. Provide each team with a heavy blanket, strong enough to bear the weight of one person. One member of each team is chosen to play the role of the casualty case.

Each injured player goes to a specified area about one hundred yards away. The other four members on each team wait at the starting goal.

When the signal to begin is given, each team runs with its own blanket to pick up its injured player. The blanket is stretched out on the ground, and the casualty case is placed on it. Then the four members of the team take a corner of the stretcher and carry their teammate back to the goal. The first group back is declared champion rescue unit.

51. WIVES IN PURSUIT

Here is quite a hilarious race for married couples. Give each husband and wife team a broom and line them up at a starting point. The husbands race off first with their wives right behind. The object of the race is that couples run together, the husband allowing his wife to stay close enough to constantly tap him on the head with the straw end of the broom. If he gets too far ahead, the team is disqualified. Both run as fast as possible in an attempt to be first to reach the finishing line.

52. PUNTING

This game can be played on a regulation football field

or similar open area. Divide players into teams. One team is designated as the kickoff team, and comes to the twenty yard line. Its most talented kicker punts the ball, attempting to gain as much distance as he can.

Whoever on the opposite team catches the ball may advance three steps and kick it again. Then someone on the other team catches the ball and repeats the action. If the ball is fumbled or strikes the ground before someone has caught it, it must be grounded. The player retrieving it can not advance three steps.

If the ball is kicked out of bounds, it must be brought in at the exact point where it went out. The team's best kicker may be the one to kick it back.

A touchdown is scored whenever one team succeeds in kicking the ball over the opposite team's goal line, regardless of whether or not that team catches the ball when it falls behind the goal line. Extra points are earned by kicking from the same point at which the touchdown was scored.

53. COMMUTER'S RELAY

Contestants are divided into two or more teams with the same number on each. The first member of every team is given a hat and topcoat. As soon as the signal has been given, each contestant races toward an opposite goal, putting on the coat and hat as he runs along. He must have them both on with the coat buttoned before he reaches the opposite side and before he may begin the trip back. As he returns, he must take off the hat and coat, and hand them to the second contestant waiting on his team, who becomes the next "commuter" in the race.

54. Sack Hop

Guests are divided into two teams with the contestants numbered on each. Teams are given a burlap bag. Line up the teams and place a stick or similar object in the center of the playing area.

The game leader calls a number, and the two members having it must put their feet into the sack and hop toward the stick. The first one there takes it back to his team, while another replaces it. The team collecting the most "trophies" wins.

55. Backward Kick

Using a football or soccer ball, see which contestant is able to kick farthest by kicking the ball so it goes back over his head rather than forward.

56. Disappearing Ice Toss

This game will provide a lot of fun for a summertime outing. Divide guests into two or more teams, with at least six on each team. Give each team a small cake of ice, identical in weight. The ice is to be passed from player to player and worked over in the hands like a bar of soap.

The winning team is that one which first makes its ice completely disappear. If anyone drops the ice and breaks it, his team is either out of the game or must take another cake of ice, whichever you decide.

57. Tire Race

Make up teams and have them line up single file at a

designated starting line. Give each team an old automobile tire. At the go signal, the first member of each team must roll the tire to a goal point, such as a large rock or tree, circle this object and return. As soon as he gets back, the next number on his team takes the tire over the same route.

58. RACING ON STILTS

Using a few pieces of old lumber, construct a pair of identical stilts. Be sure they are designed so that anyone who begins to fall may leap to safety. To add a bit more fun to the race, place some obstacles in the path to be crossed. A contestant is not disqualified if he loses his balance, but can get back on to continue.

59. BALLOON RELAY RACE

Use two or more teams for this shuttle relay. Half of the runners stand on one goal line, with the other half on the opposite side. Give each team a balloon.

At the signal to go, the first contestant on each team begins to run, batting the balloon in the air. He must not catch the balloon, but keep tapping it ahead with his hands. He brings the balloon down to his teammate at the other goal, who then takes the balloon and bats it back to the opposite side.

60. LAST COUPLE OUT

This is an old favorite enjoyed outdoors during the

warm weather season. Players are divided into two couples,
a boy and a girl or a man and woman, if possible. Someone starts the game as "it" and stands at the front with
his back to the other players. Couples stand behind "it,"
keeping a straight line, with each couple standing side by
side.

"It" calls "Last couple out!" This is the signal for the
couple at the end of the line to separate, the man around
his side of the line, moving forward, while the woman
does the opposite on her side of the line. The idea is that
they must both run beyond the one who is it, and join
hands before either of them can be tagged.

If "it" succeeds in touching either of them, he becomes
the partner of the woman member of the team, while
the man becomes "it" for another round.

61. ONE-LEGGED COMBAT

Here is a contest for men only. Divide male guests into
two teams and get them lined up for combat. Each contestant stands on one leg, holding the other foot in his hand.
Balancing on just one leg, he tries to see how many on the
opposing team he is able to knock off balance.

When someone falls or is forced to put down his raised
foot, he is disqualified. The team which disqualifies all the
members of the other team is the winner.

62. BUBBLE GUM CONTEST

Each contestant is given a large stick of bubble gum.
At the signal to begin, each unwraps the gum, pops it into
his mouth and attempts to blow the largest bubble.

Station a committee of judges nearby to decide on a winner. Or you could have each contestant stand with both hands behind his back as he tries to be the first to blow six bubbles in a row. This will be a bit difficult, as no one will be able to use his hands to get the bubble back into his mouth for the next blow.

63. TWENTY-FIVE STEP DASH

Line up racers behind a starting point and allow each to take twenty-five giant steps before he must stop. The contestant who has traveled the greatest distance in taking his twenty-five steps wins the race.

64. KICKING BASKETBALL

Use an old basketball or soccer ball for this game. Follow standard baseball rules except that you do not use a pitcher. When a player comes to bat, he kicks the ball. It is then fielded just as in regular baseball.

65. POTATO GOLF

Map out a very small golf course with only a few feet for any of the greens. Then supply each golfer with a club and potato and get the game underway.

66. Men to the Left

This softball game should give the women a decided
advantage over the men. The game is played on an even
basis, except that all men must throw left-handed (unless
this is the hand they normally use). In addition, the men
must hold the bat on the opposite side of their usual
position at plate. Switch hitters may use only one hand
on the bat.

67. Balloon Messages

This contest calls for a good deal of team work and can
be played either outdoors or inside.

Prepare a series of instructions on slips of paper. Relate the messages grouped together so each series of instructions can be followed by the members of a team.
Fold the slips and place them inside balloons.

When the teams have been divided and given their
balloons, signal them to begin. Contestants must blow
up the balloons until each breaks, so they can get their
instructions.

Team members collect the directions, and as soon as
they have them all, they follow them. Instructions guide
the teams as to where they must go and what must be
done. The first team through wins.

68. Back to Back

Have contestants pick partners. Each pair stands back

to back, while their ankles are tied together. Line up the handicapped runners, and instruct them to make their way toward a goal line, keeping their arms hooked together.

69. LOBSTER RACE

Mark off a goal line and race contestants on their hands and knees. Everyone must progress either backward or sideways. Anyone who goes head first is disqualified.

70. DRINKING CUP

Each contestant is given a paper cup half filled with water. At the signal to go, contestants race to the finish line with their cups, turn and face the starting line. They must then kneel down, place the cup between their teeth, and with their hands behind their backs, drink all the water with the cup held firmly in their teeth. When their cups are empty, they race back to the starting line.

71. THE PRINCE AND CINDERELLA

This is a good picnic contest for teenagers and adults. Have the women choose male partners. The girls then sit down at a starting line and take off both shoes. The shoes are moved to another line about thirty feet away, where all the shoes are mixed up in a pile. When the signal is given

to begin, boys run to the pile of shoes, find the pair belonging to their partner and return to the starting line where
they must put the shoes back on.

72. Scalping Party

Give each contestant a paper sack just large enough to
fit snugly on top of his head. At the signal to begin, each
player tightens the sack securely down on his head. From
then on, he may not touch it during the rest of the competition.

Contestants scatter around the "battlefield" and attempt
to grab as many scalps as possible without losing their
own. As soon as another warrior does steal his sack, however, that "scalped" player is out of the game.

73. Shuttle Relay

Make up two evenly numbered teams of ice skaters, and
line half of each team on one goal, with the second half
at an opposite line. The first skater from each team races
across to the opposite side, touches the hand of his teammate, who then skates back. This is repeated until everyone has raced and one team is declared the winner. Or,
you might have each team on the same goal line and instruct skaters to race to a goal line, circle it, and then
return to the team before the next skater can start out.

74. Slippery Tug of War

Conduct a regular tug of war on the ice. It will be

much more difficult for contestants to gain a sure footing as they pull for their side.

75. Broom Skid

Contestants compete in this race by pairs. Give each team an old broom. One player sits on the straw end, holding on to the broom handle. His partner pulls him over the ice to an opposite goal. When they reach this goal, they switch places and race back to the starting line. Be sure the rider keeps his feet still and does not assist in any way with speed.

76. Single Skate Race

Conduct a race with contestants wearing a skate on only one foot. They start off from a line at a signal, propelling themselves across the racing area.

77. Handicap Skating Race

Line up races and give each an identical object which must be carried across the ice to the finish line. Some handicaps might be a pile of logs, an open umbrella, or even a large snow ball.

PART THREE

●
●
●

WALL TO WALL FUN

A host or hostess with a good assortment of indoor games is well on the way toward a successful adult party. If a game is interesting, amusing, or challenging, even the most sophisticated grownup can lose himself in the fun of group participation.

Many of the games included in this section follow a Bible theme and would be especially appropriate for church-related activities. As with any group activity, the wise game leader should develop a keen sixth sense in determining when to abandon one game or contest and introduce a new one. Keep the game schedule varied as well as flexible, and your guests will find themselves surrounded with wall to wall fun.

78. THE MAD MUSICIANS

For this brand new game, instruct about a half a dozen expected guests to bring to the party an instrument they can play. As the game gets underway, give each ten minutes to instruct a partner, who does not know how to play the instrument, in mastering just two notes from a familiar tune. Mark out ahead of time on the sheet music, so each "teacher" knows just which two notes he will be responsible for teaching.

It might be a good idea to go ahead with another quick game or stunt while the music lessons are in progress.

At the end of the time limit, players reassemble in proper order according to the notes they have learned. Led by their instructors, each gives the two notes they have learned in order to make up the line from the tune. If not enough instruments are available, you can give two additional players two notes to hum.

79. CANDLE RACE

This colorful game should be played in a room where there is no danger of fire. Contestants are divided into pairs with a man and a woman on each team.. The men stand in a line at one end of the room, each holding an unlighted candle. The women are placed at the opposite end of the room and given a match. The lights are turned out, and a signal given to begin.

The women must light their matches, then race across the room to light each teammate's candle. If any woman's match goes out while she is running, she must return to get another match and light it.

The first to light her teammate's candle wins, but encourage the other runners to finish, as a lovely effect is
created by the moving light.

80. AUTOBIOGRAPHY

Here is a new game that will help guests become better acquainted as well as introduce interesting topics for
conversation. Instruct each guest to write a one para-
graph description of an incident that occurred at some
time in his life. Make it in some way unique and an indi-
cation of individual personality.

Then give each guest a sheet of paper to list names of
guests as the sketches are read aloud in an attempt to
identify the person involved in the event.

81. BABY GALLERY

If possible, arrange before the party to have guests
bring a baby picture of themselves. Number the pictures
and tape them on display for an amusing guessing game.
Allow players to view each of the numbered pictures and
then list as many identifications as possible. The person
with the most correct listing in a designated time is the
winner.

82. CONTEST IN HUMILITY

Pin six ribbons on the collar of each guest and tell him
that for the next fifteen minutes, he must not use the word

"I." Any guest caught referring to himself this way must hand over one ribbon to the first player who points out his mistake. The person who has gathered the most ribbons at the end' of the game receives a prize.

83. WALK THE TIGHT ROPE

Stretch out a length of string and give each guest an opportunity to walk the rope, looking down at his progress through the large end of a pair of binoculars.

84. SEND A TELEGRAM

Divide guests into two or more teams, and stand each team in a line. Have identical messages made out in advance and sealed in envelopes—one for each team.

When the signal is given to begin, the first contestant on each team tears open the envelope and quickly reads through the message. He must then crumple up the paper, throw it on the floor, turn to the next person in line and whisper the message. That person repeats it to the next member on his team and so on down the line. The last person runs to the judge and whispers the message to him. (Be sure the judge has been provided with an exact copy of the message.)

First prize should go to the team able to relay the telegram most accurately. This might not necessarily be the first team in. Make the messages a bit difficult to pass from mouth to mouth, but not longer than a dozen words. The telegram could relate that refreshments are being served, or perhaps introduce the next activity.

85. Sundae Extravaganza

Set up a table with as wide an assortment of toppings, fruits, nuts, and small paper decorations as can be managed. Then pass around large bowls of ice cream to each guest, instructing them to be creative. Award a prize for the most unusual or attractive sundae, *after* its creator has managed to down it all himself.

86. Blindfolded Candle Blow

A good game to introduce to a group of adults. One player is chosen to hold a lighted candle. Another is blindfolded and brought to the candle, where he is given ten chances to blow it out. If the candle is still burning after ten tries, the blower changes places with the candle holder and he tries ten times. After each of these has had a turn, two other players try to blow it out.

87. Whose Nose?

Make a hole in an old sheet, just large enough for contestants to put their noses through. Have six or eight volunteers display their noses in turn, while the other players attempt identification. It is permissable to touch the nose and carefully examine it before a guess is made.

88. Best Foot Forward

A good adaption of the nose identification is to have

players remove their shoes and poke one bare foot out from behind a screen or similar shield, as the other contestants attempt to guess the person whose foot they can see.

89. LOONEY LINE UP

Here is a new game that will introduce some excitement and intrigue to the party game time. Ask for five or six volunteers. These players leave the room and pull a nylon stocking over their heads and faces. With a sheet wrapped tightly around each "suspect," the lineup moves across a lighted area as the other players attempt to list in order the guests they think are on parade.

90. LIVING ART

For a change in the game activity, conduct a modern art show with teams of five or more using arms and legs in weird arrangements to compose a modern art object.

91. LEMON RELAY

Players are divided into two equal groups for the lemon relay. The first player in each group is given a pencil and a lemon. After a starting point and goal have been marked off with chalk on the floor, each player, using a pencil, must roll the lemon to the goal and back. The next player in his group then takes his turn until all have finished.

92. Customs Inspection

Put a different object in each of several paper bags and staple them closed. Guests are seated in a circle and, as the bags are passed from player to player, list their guess at the contents of each. Be sure to have the sacks carefully numbered.

93. Ankles Away

This is a new game that will be enjoyed by teenage party guests as well as adults. The game leader takes one long length of string and, in criss-cross fashion, ties together the ankles of each team member. The first team to successfully untangle itself without breaking the string wins.

For fairness sake, be sure to use the identical pattern for each team.

94. Balance the Ice Cube

Give each racer a table knife and an ice cube, and line everyone at a starting point. The object of the race is that runners must keep the ice cube balanced on the knife. When it slips off, the runner must slide it back on the knife without using his fingers.

95. Balloon Stomp

Tie a balloon to both ankles of each contestant. Every-

one clasps hands to form a circle. Without letting go of
hands, each guest attempts to break the balloons of those
around him by stamping on them. If both of his balloons
are broken, a contestant must drop out of the circle. The
last two with at least one unbroken balloon win.

This can also be played with each contestant free to
move about in individual conquest.

96. PING PONG BALL RACE

Line up two guests at one end of the room and provide each with a straw and a ping pong ball. Stretch a
string across the opposite end of the room. Contestants get
down on the floor and, using only their straws for loco-
motion, blow the ball across the string line.

97. HANDKERCHIEF KEEPAWAY

This is a fast moving game which can be played indoors
without fear of damage to floor or furniture.

Players are seated in a circle, facing inward. Keep the
circle of chairs tight. One player is selected as "it" and
placed in the center of the circle.

The players toss a handkerchief from one to another
across and around their circle. "It" attempts to touch the
handkerchief. When he succeeds, the player who last
touched the handkerchief becomes next to be "it." Urge
players to get rid of the handkerchief quickly, and keep it
moving.

98. BIOGRAPHY TRUE OR FALSE

Here is a new game that will serve well to introduce a new pastor or youth director to teenagers or adults. Conduct an interview prior to the get-together and secure some pertinent information about the subject. Use this to compose a list of twenty statements—some true, a few false—about the new personality. After the game, be sure to distinguish which facts are true, which are not.

99. FLOWERPOT

A game for junior aged children, teenagers, and adults. Players are seated in a circle, with one of them having been sent from the room while the others think of some activity. The absent player returns and questions anyone he chooses. Answers must be given truthfully. In asking the questions, the word flowerpot is used to represent the activity. If, for example, the players have chosen "diving," the questions might be. "Do you flowerpot in the house?" Or perhaps, "How many people can flowerpot at the same time?" Is it fun to flowerpot?" etc. In answering questions, players also use the word flowerpot. Questioning continues until the activity has been named, with the first person answering when the activity was guessed being next to leave the room while a new activity is chosen.

100. COTTON THROW

A good contest for an indoor party is to have players

throw large balls of soft, fluffy cotton. Designate a mark behind which each pitcher must stand, and then see who can throw his cotton ball farthest.

101. Banana Gobble

Each contestant is given a banana. At the signal, each must peel his banana and eat it, keeping one hand behind his back at all times.

102. Living Room Basketball

Place a chair on each end of the living room and stand a guest on each chair with his arms held out to form a basketball rim. Use a toy balloon as a basketball, and follow the regular rules of the game except have no more than four on a team. Of course, the "baskets" must not move about to help catch a balloon, but must keep their arms rigid.

103. Jack O Lantern Seed Toss

You can use your party jack o lantern and its seeds for a colorful Halloween contest. Make the jack o lantern from the largest pumpkin you can find and give it an over-sized round mouth.

Dry the pumpkin seeds and, at the party, give each contestant fifteen or twenty seeds. The object is to throw as many seeds as possible into the mouth of the jack o lantern.

104. CHAMPIONSHIP SHOOT

For this contest, a cork-shooting toy gun is needed. A target is prepared by fastening a clothespin to a tight wire line. Attach a piece of cardboard to one side of the top of the pin. When a target is hit, the clothespin will spin around and fall off the wire. Award prizes based on the number of successful hits.

105. PEAS ON A KNIFE

Fill two bowls with an equal number of dried peas and place them on the opposite side of the room from two empty bowls. Divide guests into two teams, and give the first member of each team a table knife.

At the signal to go, the first member of each team scoops his knife into his team's bowl, then picks up as many peas on the knife as he can. He carries these across to the empty bowl at the opposite goal, and races back to hand the knife to the next contestant in line, who repeats the procedure.

Play continues until all of the players from each team have had a chance to transport the dried peas. The team which has managed to transfer the most peas from one bowl across to the other is declared winner. Peas which have fallen along the way are not counted and can not be retrieved as the contestants move along.

106. CATCH THE CAN IF YOU CAN

For this contest, a number of different sized tin cans are nailed to a board, with the open end tilting out. Each

can is given a different number value. Points are earned by
tossing bottle caps into the cans.

107. TARGET PRACTICE

Attach a comical false face to the handle of a broom
and lean it up against the wall. Each player is allowed
three tries to hit the broom in the face, causing it to fall.
Any type of ball can be used for the target practice.

108. EYE SPY

As the party gets underway, guests are given paper and
pencil and instructed that there are pictures, appropriate to
the occasion of the party, posted about the room. Each
picture is numbered. Players must list as many objects as
they can find in each picture that begin with a certain
letter, such as C or B. Award a prize to the contestant
coming up with the longest list after a set time limit.

109. MATCH THIS

Each player is given an empty pop bottle and a large
box of kitchen matches. Players begin by laying four
matches across the open top of the bottle, two over two.
Then they proceed in turn to lay one match at a time,
building the pile higher and wider before it finally col-
lapses.

110. Goblet Symphony

A thin water goblet can be made to "sing" beautifully when you rub its edge with the flat of a finger. Fill glasses with varying amounts of water to produce different notes and have guests work out a tune.

111. Dizzy Relay

Divide players into two or more teams. Give each team a stick about four feet long. As the race gets underway, each team member takes his stick across to a goal point. When he gets there, he positions the stick perpendicular to the ground, places his hands on the upright end of the stick, puts his head on hands, and turns around quickly ten times. After he has done this, he'll no doubt be quite dizzy, but must pick up the stick and run back to hand it to the next contestant on his team.

112. Tight Wire Wrestling

Two contestants face each other and touch the toes of their right feet. Each then places his left foot directly behind the right one, toes touching heels. The two clasp right hands and attempt to wrestle each other out of that position, forcing the movement of either front of back foot.

113. Shoe Scramble

This game is most fun when there are a great many

participants to add to the confusion. Each player removes both shoes and puts them in a basket. The basket is then carried some distance away. At a signal, contestants make a dash for the collection. The first to get his own shoes back on and return to the starting point is the winner.

114. BLINDFOLD PILLOW FIGHT

Secure volunteers for a few rounds of pillow fighting. Pair off contestants and, as they enter the ring, each is blindfolded. Hang a small bell around the neck of each fighter, so that opponents will be able to locate one another in the ring. Encourage a great deal of ringside applause to add to the fun.

115. PEANUT TREASURE HUNT

Sometime before party guests arrive, hide a number of unshelled peanuts around the living room in places not too difficult to find.

When the game starts, divide guests into two sides, the cats and the cows, with a team leader for each. Instruct each guest that, when he locates a peanut, he must kneel down on the spot and make the noise his team represents until the team leader can come to collect the nut.

Participants cannot take the peanuts to their leader, but must continue mooing or meowing until he comes to them.

After five minutes or so have passed, halt the game and have the total number of collected peanuts counted to determine which team has won.

116. Newspaper Race

Give each contestant two sheets of newspaper and line them up for the race. The idea is to move as rapidly across the racing area as possible by putting first one sheet of paper down and stepping on it while another is laid down for the next foot. Have racers move toward a goal line, turn and come back to the starting point.

117. Miniature Soccer

Here is a new indoor adaption of soccer that will be enjoyed by teenage fellows as well as the older men, perhaps while the ladies are preparing refreshments.

Use a toy balloon for the ball and position teams in the same manner as for a regular game, except that players get down on all fours to blow the balloon across the playing area.

No body contact is permitted. If a player is fouled, his team is allowed one free blow toward the goal.

118. Whistle Serenade

Divide players into teams with two on a team—men and women if the group is composed of couples. Line up the women at one end of the room and give each a pencil and paper. Give the men a sealed envelope containing a slip of paper with the title of a well-known song.

Line up the men opposite the room from their partners. When the signal is given, each man races across to his partner and, when he has touched her outstretched hand, he is allowed to open the envelope, discover the song title and whistle or hum as much of it as necessary until the girl is able to recognize it. As soon as she thinks she can, she writes the title on the piece of paper she has been holding, and the man checks to be sure it is right before racing back to the goal line.

Station a judge at both goals to be sure no one slips and tells the song title to his partner and to check the titles for accuracy.

119. COMPARED TO ME

The group decides together on an object in plain sight in the room but unknown to "it." He must attempt to guess the article by asking each player to, "compare it to me." If the article is a plant, a typical exchange might be. "The object is like you because it is alive." Another might add, "It is like you because it enjoys the sun." The player giving the last comparison before it correctly guesses is "it" for the next round.

120. MULTIPLE WORDS

The leader gives one player a word. Within one minute, the player calls out as many words as he can think of beginning with the first letter of the word named. If this is played as a team game, limit the time allowed to only half a minute for each player on the team, scoring one point for every word named.

121. ALPHABET GAME

Before the party, prepare twenty-six cards with one letter of the alphabet printed clearly on each. The cards are mixed up, and the game leader shows them, one by one, to the group. The players have already decided on what type of object the letters will represent These could be grocery items, flowers, birds, etc.

When a letter is held up, the first player to call out an item in the correct category beginning with that letter is given the card. At the conclusion of the game, the player holding the most cards is leader for the next game.

If several words are called out at the same time, that card is returned to be shown later.

122. LYRICS

The leader gives each player a different word allowing one minute to think of a song in which that word appears. Each player must be ready to give a line from a song when he is called on. This can also be played as a team game, with the leader giving each team three different words and a brief time to think of three songs in which each appears.

123. DUCK SHOOT

Float several plastic ducks, or other children's bath toys, in a large tub of water. Give each "hunter" six or eight rubber canning jar rings and see who can shoot the most ducks from a distance of about five feet.

124. Powers of Observation

Have guests make a careful survey of the living room, then send them all into an adjoining room. Make several alterations in the vacated room, being careful to note these carefully on a list. Bring the guests back and give each a pencil and paper with the instructions to write down all the changes they can notice.

Some typical alterations might be to open the drapes, move a lamp, upturn a vase, etc.

125. Time Flies

Draw a number of clock faces, showing various times of the day, and hide these around the house. When it is time for the game, instruct the guests what they are searching for. Award a prize to the person finding the most clocks and to the one whose times add up to the highest figure. Set the times on the hour and half hour, and in adding up the score, begin counting at one o'clock.

126. Blow the Feather

Divide guests into equally numbered teams and give each team a small feather. As the game gets underway, each team tosses its feather into the air and tries to keep it up by blowing. All contestants must keep their hands locked behind their backs.

The team which can keep its feather in the air longest is declared winner.

127. COORDINATION

Divide contestants into teams with two on a team. Taking turns, each team attempts a ring toss in the following manner. One contestant holds a broom, keeping his foot on the straws so that the bottom never moves. He is allowed to move the stick portion back and forth as much as possible without moving the bottom. His partner stands about ten feet away and tosses a dozen rubber rings at the broom. The stick is moved about in an attempt to catch as many as possible.

128. NUTTY NEWSCAST

Here's a new game in which each player is given three different slips of paper indicating three locations or persons in the world. Players read their slips and then wait in a long row while one player, good at ad-libing, starts a nutty newscast. He refers to a list indicating locations and personalities to include. As he mentions some activity in a location, or a personality, all players holding those slips must race to a designated T.V. screen area and attempt to pantomine the circumstances being reported.

129. CORN TOSS

Contestants are given ten kernals of corn or corn candy to toss into a small box placed on a table about four feet away. Score ten points for each kernal landing inside the box.

130. Mimic

Guests are seated in a circle with "it" in the center, eyes closed, as a leader is chosen. Everyone else follows the actions of the leader.

As "it" opens his eyes, the leader begins some motion with his hands such as clapping, moving up and down, snapping his fingers, and the others mimic him. The point of the game is that when "it" is not looking, the leader switches to another gesture, and everyone changes with him. "It" must keep watching around the circle until he can determine who is initiating new movements. Then "it" and the leader change places and a new leader is chosen.

131. Turtle Race

Here is a game which is proving to be quite popular and will add variety to the party. Cut from heavy cardboard as many turtle shapes as will be raced. These should be about twelve inches long and proportioned in width. Punch a small hole in the back of the turtle, about one-fourth of the distance from its head and about three-fourth distance from its tail, exactly in the center from its sides at that point and run a long string through the hole.

Two contestants are assigned to each turtle. One stands holding a string close to the floor at the point where the turtle begins, the other stands with his foot on the opposite end of the string some thirty feet away.

When the signal is given to begin, that contestant nearest the turtle begins jiggling the string sideways and up and down, whichever proves most feasible for him, endeavoring to keep his turtle hopping along the race course. At no time may the turtle leave the floor, though he may stand upright, lean sideways, or skim along close to the surface of the floor. When the turtle reaches the opposite side, that contestant picks up the string, while the other puts his end of the string under his feet, and the turtle is returned across the racing area. Do not attempt to race the turtles over a carpeted area.

132. Ring Race

A modification of the above game is to have a ring placed on each string, and contestants then try to move the ring across the string. Hand height must be between waist and shoulders of each participant.

133. Initial Story

Players select two initials, such as "b" and "s." The leader begins a story of a person having those initials. Everything describing him or what he sees or does must be a combination of the two initials in their correct order. An example would be the tale of blonde, sweet, Bessie Smith, who lives in a beautiful, small house. She awakens one morning, blowing and sniffling. Each player is given an opportunity to add a new fact to the yarn, which can continue around the group as many times as you wish.

134. Bible Name Contest

Divide the group into two teams and line them up as for

a spelling match. The leader of one side will begin the game by calling out the first syllable in the name of a Bible character. The leader of the opposing team will complete the name if possible. Should he be unable to, he must drop out of the game and the contestant giving that syllable completes the word while the teammate next in line on his side gives the first syllable of a new word and challenges the opposing team to finish it. In other words, first one side and then the other gives a syllable and finishes a a word.

135. Pass the Grapefruit

Divide players into two or more teams of equal number, and line each team in single file. The first member on each team is given a grapefruit to place under his chin, clamping it there without using his hands. As the signal to begin is given, he must turn and pass the grapefruit to the team member standing behind him without either of them handling the fruit.

If the grapefruit is dropped, it must be picked up by the player who had it last, placed back in position under his chin and then passed on again. This continues until the end of the line is reached and one team declared winner.

136. Occupation Pantomine

When guests are not familiar with one another, this is a good game to help them become better acquainted. Divide guests into teams. One group remains seated, while each member of the other takes his turn to pantomine the actions associated with his occupation.

As soon as a person's occupation has been correctly identified, he sits down. When all the jobs have been guessed on the first team, the second team gets up for a try.

137. MOTHER GOOSE PANTOMINE

Allow teams five minutes to prepare a pantomine based on a well-known nursery rhyme theme. Every member of the team must be included in the cast. One group performs for the other, while that one attempts to guess. The audience should allow the other team to complete its performance before venturing a guess.

138. INITIAL DESCRIPTION

Try this game based on the three initials of the guest at a birthday party. The object of the game is to have a three sentence answer from every player, each word beginning with the initials in proper order of the person whose birthday is being celebrated. If his name is Robert A. Delton, for example, possible questions and answers might be:

1. What sort of person is he? (Rough and devious)
2. Where does he live? (Rustic, antique doghouse)
3. What are his favorite food? (Radishes, avacodos, dumplings)
4. What is his greatest ambition? (Ride a dinosaur)
5. What are his hobbies? (Roses, airplanes, diving)

139. How, When, Where and Why

One person is chosen to leave the room while the remaining group chooses a noun article. When the player returns, he attempts to learn the correct noun by asking questions of the other players, such as, "When do you like it? How do you like it? Where do you like it? Why do you like it?" He continues questioning, until he is able to guess the noun, or he gives up.

140. Familiar Combinations

The game leader prepares a list of well-known combinations such as salt and pepper, black and white, bacon and eggs, etc. He points to a player, calling out the first half of the combination. The player must answer with the other half before the leader can count to five. If he doesn't give the right word, the player is out of the game. Another player is pointed out and the procedure repeated until only a few players remain.

141. Jingle Bells

Guests are seated in a circle with someone chosen as "it" in the center. "It" closes his eyes and counts aloud to ten, while a small bell is passed around the circle. When the count reaches ten, "it" quickly opens his eyes and tries to decide who has the bell. By the time he reaches eight or nine, whoever has the bell then should put his hands behind him and try to keep from giving away the secret by his expression. Other guests do the same in an attempt to confuse it.

If the one holding the bell is correctly guessed, it changes places with the person caught. If not, the game is repeated.

142. SPINNING A YARN

Have a number of pieces of string of approximately equal length. Give each guest a string and seat all in a line. Get the "yarn" underway by having someone begin a tale. As he continues the story, he winds up his length of string. When he pauses, he must stop winding the string until he starts again.

When he has wound his portion, he gives the ball to the next person in line who attaches his own string to the end and begins winding. As he does, he picks up the story where it was left by the last storyteller. This procedure continues on down the line.

It might be a good idea to caution guests that, as the ball nears the end, they should begin bringing the yarn to a logical conclusion, with the last person in line using the time it takes to wind up his length of string to wind up the story.

143. CONTINUED STORY

Another interesting game of storytelling involves seating guests in a circle on the floor. One of the players acts as the leader, and it is up to him to call out "stop" at any point in the course of the game, once the story has begun. When he does this, the next person in line must pick up the story exactly where it was halted and continue until the command to stop is again given. The story might possibly be related as the humorous biography of some honored guest at the gathering.

144. PARTNER PACKAGE WRAP

For an interesting contest, divide guests into couples—preferably a man and a woman in each pair. Each couple gets a box or some large, bulky object, some newspaper and string with instructions to wrap the package.

The difficulty arises when you also inform them that one partner must work with his left hand behind his back, while his partner must keep his right hand out of the activity.

145. CANDLE BLOW OUT

Place a lighted candle on a table and point out its position to the contestants. Blindfold players one at a time, give them a few turns, and send them in search of the candle. The only way they can locate the flame is to first find the table and then cautiously check the air for warmth.

When the candle has been located, the contestant attempts to be first to blow it out.

146. BROKEN HEARTS

Here is an appropriate contest for a party with a Valentine's Day theme. Give each guest a heart cut into about ten pieces, which cannot easily be fitted back together. The first contestant to mend his broken heart is the winner.

147. STIFF-LEGGED RACE

Line up contestants in two teams. Mark off a spot for the goal line and, at the signal, the first person on each team must run to the goal, keeping one leg stiff until he gets back. If he forgets to do this, he loses a point for his team. When he gets back, the second person in line on his team starts out. This is also a good game to conduct outside, using a large area.

148. ORIGINAL CREATIONS

Place a large box of miscellaneous objects such as macaroni, buttons, broken bead sets, etc., anything with a hole in it or that could be used to make original jewelry creations. Each girl contestant is given a length of string and a pair of scissors.

Allow each girl one dip into the box with both hands. Whatever she picks up in that dip is the only material she may use.

When the signal is given, contestants are allowed ten minutes in which to make any kind of jewelry they can with the material available.

149. INITIAL ALIBI

Select a question on a general topic, something that

would be appropriate to the circumstances of the group. An example might be, "Why don't you contribute five thousand dollars to our current building project?" Instruct each player to use his initials in order to come up with an alibi. Each word of the alibi must begin with the letters of his initials. A contestant with the initials NMC might answer, "Not Much Cash."

150. Ducks Fly

One person chosen to be game leader stands in front of the other players. He begins by saying, "ducks fly," and waving his arms in a flying motion. Immediately the other members of the group respond by imitating his action because it is true that ducks do fly.

However, if he should say, "dogs fly," the others must not respond, even though the leader will attempt to fool them by again making a flying motion. If he says, "dogs run," and begins a running action, the others do the same. In other words, the leader's actions are followed when he speaks the truth, ignored when he contradicts it.

The first player to respond in error is the new leader. If more than one player makes the mistake, a leader is chosen from them, or those players may be disqualified from the game.

151. Lots of Cents

Place two chairs at one end of the room and line up two teams opposite them on the other end. Put a paper plate on each chair and another with one penny for each contestant near each team.

Each player is given a drinking straw and, at the signal to go, the first member in line runs to the plate, sucks up a penny on the end of his straw, and carries it to the plate on the other end of the room. If he drops it, he is disqualified.

152. MINIATURE VOLLEYBALL

Volleyball enthusiasts can play this game on the living room floor when weather conditions keep them indoors. Use a large inflated balloon for a volleyball and line up several chairs to serve as nets. Play follows regular rules, except contestants remain on their knees at all times.

153. MAN OR MAID

Here is a game that will provide a lot of laughs. Seat the players in a circle, with one player blindfolded in the center. Blindfolded "it" goes to stand before one of the seated guests and asks, "Are you a man or a maid?" That person must answer in a disguised voice or whisper, "That is for you to guess."

"It" attempts to guess. If he is correct, the two change places. If he has guessed wrong, he moves on to try someone else.

154. DONUT GOBBLE

Line up five volunteers at one end of the room. At the

other end, place five chairs in a row. On each chair, put a
paper plate with a messy powdered sugar donut on it.
When the signal is given, contestants race to the chairs, eat
the donut without using either hand, and then run back to
the starting point. The first one back wins a prize.

155. EGG CARTON TOSS

Guests are divided into teams of five or more each, according to the size of the group. Place an empty egg carton
six feet in front of the leader of each team.

Each contestant receives seven marbles. As the signal to
begin is given, leaders attempt to throw as many of their
marbles as possible into the egg cartons. When they have
thrown all their marbles, the next team member steps into
position for his turn. Play continues until each player has
thrown all of his marbles. Award each team a point for every
marble that remained in the carton.

156. WIND UP RACE

Divide contestants into pairs and equip each team with
a string of identical length, with a small stick attached to
each end. At a given signal, both contestants begin winding
the string on to the stick. The first couple to reach each
other is declared the winner.

157. BUCKET BRIGADE

Divide guests into two or more teams of equal number

and provide each member of a team with a paper cup. Each team has two milk or juice bottles (same size bottle for each team). One of the bottles is filled with water and placed at one end of the line, with the empty bottle situated at the opposite end.

When a signal is given, the first member of each team fills his cup with water from the bottle. He then pours this water into the cup of the contestant next to his. This contestant pours the water from his cup into that of his neighbor, and so on down the line until the last contestant empties his cup into the empty bottle on that end. This continues until one team has emptied the full bottle, cup by cup, down the line to the other bottle.

158. CANDLE RELAY

Teams are arranged in parallel lines. Equip the first player on each team with a candle and a package of matches. When a signal is given, he lights the candle, runs to a goal, then returns to his team, and gives the lighted candle to the second runner.

If the candle should go out during the race, the runner must stop and relight it before continuing.

159. URANIUM HUNT

For this game, you need a clock which ticks at a normal volume. Have the guests leave the room while the clock is hidden. Then play music softly, to partially deaden the sound of the ticking, as guests are brought into the room and told to move around in an attempt to discover the tickihg source.

You might have them stretch out one hand, geiger counter fashion.

As soon as each guest thinks he has located the clock, he comes to the game leader to whisper this information. If correct, he may sit down. Otherwise, he must continue the uranium hunt.

160. THREAD THE NEEDLE

Here is a challenging game for husbands and wives. Place all the husbands on one goal line, with their wives situated across the room. Give each man a piece of thread and give his wife a needle.

At the signal to go, husbands race to the opposite goal, where the wives are waiting with a needle. Without any help from his wife, each husband must thread the needle as his wife holds it. When he succeeds in getting the needle properly threaded, he runs back to the goal. The first husband to arrive back with his threaded needle is declared sewing champion.

161. MUSICAL COUNT DOWN

Divide guests into two sides. Someone at the piano plays excerpts of hymns. The first contestant to correctly name the hymn earns one point for his team. As soon as a contestant has earned five points, he must sit down, since some guests are certain to be more familiar with music than others.

easoffrt3/rasnig_ffrt

162. Bean Pass

Before starting this contest, put aside a number of beans that can easily be held at the end of a soda straw when someone sucks up on the opposite end. Divide the guests into teams of equal number, providing each contestant with a straw.

Start a bean down each line by having the first member attach a bean to the end of his straw, holding it there without using his hands.

When the go signal is given, the first contestant holds out the bean at the end of his straw and has the next member of his team take it off the end of the straw by sucking it onto his own. No hands may be used. Should the bean drop, it must be replaced on the straw of the last team member to have it.

This continues through to the end of the line, with the first team finished declared champion bean passers.

163. Verse or Chorus

Conduct a spell down around favorite hymns. Instruct a pianist to play brief excerpts from a hymn. The contestants must tell whether the portion played is part of a verse or a chorus.

164. Rotation Ping Pong

Here is a good game to play when you have a large number of ping pong enthusiasts, but only one ping pong table. Organize the group into teams of equal number. The

game is played by regular ping pong rules, except that
players line up in single file.

When one player has served the ball, he moves quickly
out of the way. When the ball is returned, the second player
in line moves to position. When the ball comes back again,
the third player is there.

Meanwhile, players who have had their turn go back to
the end of the line to play again.

165. DUMB DUMB CRAMBO

Guests are divided into two groups, with one group being sent from the room while the remaining group picks a
verb. When the opposing team returns, they are told a verb
that rhymes with the chosen verb.

For example, suppose the verb "kick" is selected. The
group is informed that a rhyming verb is flick. After that,
no words are spoken. Instead, the guessing group acts out
various possible verbs such as lick, slick, trick, until it hits
on the kicking verb action.

When this occurs, players from group one give them a
loud cheer. Group number two then takes a turn deciding
on a verb to be identified.

166. LOST COUPLES

This game is a good one to include at an adult party, but
is enjoyed by children as well.

Choose three or four couples, and give each couple a like
object to hold. Both members of one couple might carry a

toothbrush and each member of another couple might hold a pen.

Blindfold the couples and scatter them widely about the room, instructing that no one may speak. As they grope about the room, each person must attempt to locate his partner. He does this by contacting someone and attempting to determine whether or not that person carries the same object he does.

Spectators may enter the playing area now and then to confuse the blindfolded searchers and add to the fun.

As couples locate one another, they quietly remove their blinds and wait until all are matched.

167. Shoe Toss

Provide each contestant with half a dozen old shoes, and position him ten feet from a large container. Allow a few practice throws, then blindfold him and have him attempt to land as many shoes as possible in the basket or box.

168. Noah's Ark

Before this game begins, each lady selects a partner. The leader then names each couple after two of the animals that went into Noah's ark. Animals should be selected making noises the two can easily imitate—horses, sheep, ducks, dogs, etc.

The gentlemen now leave the room, while the ladies switch positions. In a separate room, the men are carefully blindfolded and led back to the room where their partners have begun making the noise of the animal each represents.

The ladies stand behind chairs and the men are supposed to find the chair in front of their partner—no simple task, as they will not be able to see and must stumble around listening for their partner's peculiar sound above the din of animal imitations.

A prize may be awarded the first successful duo to rematch with a booby prize for the last.

169. PING PONG BALL RACE

Contestants line up a starting point. As the signal to go is given, racers get down on hands and knees and blow a ping pong ball in front of them, across the room. The first one to hit the opposite wall with his ping pong ball wins. Caution contestants they may not touch the ball in any way but must only blow it across the racing area.

170. BIBLE SPELLDOWN

Conduct this contest in the same manner as a regular spelldown using names and places from the Bible. It might be wise to get underway with a few of the less complicated Bible words to spell and then proceed to more difficult words as the contest continues.

171. WORD CHAIN

Guests are seated in a circle and someone is chosen to begin the game. This person names an object. The person seated next to him names some object that is brought to mind by the one first mentioned. The third does the same and on around the circle. This can become so interesting you will want to continue several times around the circle. A typical chain might go like this. The first player says the word "train." The next says, "trip," the next, "fall," the fourth, "water," and the next, "pond," etc.

172. LYRICS, PLEASE

Guests stand in a row, while someone sits at the piano playing short excerpts from well-known hymns. Each guest takes a turn singing or reciting the lines which have been played. If anyone fails to do so, he must leave the game while play continues.

173. HIT THE DUMMY

Ask for a volunteer to stand with his back to the contestants. Designate someone to throw a bean bag, pillow, or other soft object at the "dummy."

When the dummy is hit, he turns and tries to guess who it was that hit him. If he is right, he changes positions with that person. If wrong, however, he turns his back again and another person hits him.

174. WORDS IN A BAG

Cut up small pieces of cardboard, on each of which you

print a letter from the alphabet. Place identical letters in two or more paper sacks and give each team one bag.

Announce a word which you want spelled. One at a time, contestants of each team put a hand into the sack to draw out one letter. When the letter drawn belongs in the word announced, it is placed on a table. If not, it must be returned to the bag. The first team successful in spelling out the word is winner.

175. FAKE SONGBIRD

Someone is selected to be "it," and is sent from the room. The group selects a song to sing and chooses one of the players to be the fake songbird. This player only mouths the words to the song without making any noise, while the others sing.

When "it" returns to the room, he is given two minutes to discover the silent singer. If he does, that player becomes "it." Otherwise, "it" must take another turn at guessing.

176. BIBLE TREASURE HUNT

Here is a new game, which will give your guests practice in using a Bible concordance. Each team is supplied with identical lists of objects or places located in the Bible. Instruct them that, within a designated time limit, they must locate references in which these objects are mentioned. Award a prize to each successful team.

177. HUNTING BIBLE VERSES

This game provides excellent practice in acquainting readers with the location of books in the Bible. Each player needs a Bible for this contest. The leader calls out a verse anywhere in the Bible and all immediately try to find the verse. The first one finding it correctly reads it aloud. One point is scored by a player each time he wins.

178. SILENT VOWELS

Seat players in a circle, with someone in the center who is "it."

The game begins with "it" going to anyone in the circle and giving him a simple word to spell. This person must spell the word without calling out any vowel. In place of vowels, players must lift their right hands for an A, left hand for an E, point to an eye for I, open their mouth roundly for O, point to "it" for U. All other letters of the alphabet can be spelled out loud .

When one of the players fails to use a correct sign for a vowel, he changes places and becomes "it."

179. GRAB BAG SCRABBLE

For this new game, you will need small pieces of cardboard with alphabetical letters printed clearly on them. Provide a bag of identical letters for each team playing, and be sure there are enough letters to spell out the words on a list you will be calling out.

Players are divided into teams of five or more each and are given a bag. Before a word is announced, have each player draw four letters from the team bag and decide with the other members of the team (or individually if you prefer) which three of the four letters he will keep to be held by his team in reserve.

When the teams have decided on their letters, a word is called out by the game leader. The team first able to spell out that word with the letters they have kept wins. If no team is able to spell the word, another is given. Use long words as well as short ones, and only allow one grab in which to choose letters.

180. BALLOON KICK

Give each contestant an inflated balloon and line them up along a goal line facing an opposite goal twenty or thirty yards away. When the signal is given to begin, each contestant moves forward, kicking his balloon. The object of the game is to see who can kick his balloon across the goal line first. If a balloon breaks before the goal is reached, the contestant is out of the race.

181. QUESTION AND ANSWER

Arrange players in two equal lines, facing each other. Have one person go down one line whispering a secret question into each guest's ear—a different question for each guest. Have another person whisper a different answer to each player on the opposite side.

The game proceeds with the first person on the question

team asking the question which was whispered to him, and the player seated opposite him replying with the answer he was given, no matter how unappropriate. The resulting combinations will most likely be comical, especially if the players have been given unique questions and answers.

182. Do You Like Your Neighbors?

Players are seated in a circle, with "it" in the center. "It" goes to anyone in the circle and asks him, "Do you like your neighbors?" If the person answers, "Not very well," he is asked, "Well, who would you rather have for neighbors?" The questioned player then names two other persons in the circle, who must immediately trade places with the two neighbors of the player naming them.

"It" must try to occupy one of their seats. If he is successful, the person in the middle becomes "it." Occasionally, when "it" questions a player about his neighbors, he may receive the answer, "I like my neighbors," which is the signal for everyone to change seats in a wild scramble to keep from being left without a seat.

183. Twenty Questions

Select three or four contestants, and send them from the room while the guests choose a subject or object to be identified. When the contestants return, they are told only whether the item is animal, vegetable, or mineral. Contestants are allowed a total of only twenty questions among the four of them.

The group can answer these questions with "yes" or "no." By the process of elimination, players attempt to narrow down the subject matter until they are able to reach a correct answer. With practice, a team will often be able to guess even very difficult objects within the twenty question limit.

184. BIBLE TWENTY QUESTIONS

The game of twenty questions can be used with a Bible background. Play proceeds as in the previous game, with subject matter taken from the Bible. It should be an object in most cases, rather than a person, so that its physical characteristics can be questioned in the twenty questions allowed.

185. WHO'S HUMMING

"It" stands in the middle of a circle of players. He is blindfolded and given a stick or ruler with which he leads the group in singing a hymn or chorus. At any time during the song, he may call out, "Stop," and point his baton at one of the players in the circle. That person must continue humming the melody while "it" attempts to guess his identity before he reaches the end of the song.

If "it" guesses correctly, he changes places with the player. If the group is quite small, you might give "it" only one or two tries at identifying the humming soloist.

186. PAPER PLATE TOSS

Place a wastebasket on the floor and, from a line of ten feet distance, let contestants toss paper plates into the container. Players are allowed five throws each, with successful tosses scoring one point.

187. CLOTHESPIN DROP

Place a glass milk bottle on the floor directly behind a straight-backed chair. Contestants stand on their knees on the chair and, holding the clothespins at nose level, attempt to drop as many of them as possible into the bottle. Give each player six tries, with each pin dropped into the bottle scoring ten points.

188. BALLOON BLAST

Divide players into teams, and line them up behind a starting point on one end of the room. Provide one chair for each team across the room, and give each contestant a balloon.

When the signal is given, team members take turns running across to their team chair, blowing up their balloon, and sitting down on the chair to break it.

This relay always provides a lot of fun, as some of the players are certain to experience difficulty getting their balloons broken before they can run back to the starting point.

189. WALKING ALPHABET

Guests are divided into two or more teams, with a letter
of the alphabet printed on a card given to each member of
the team. Be sure to pass out an identical selection of letters
to each team, and be certain they can spell the words you
have chosen with the letters they have been provided.

Ask Bible questions that can be answered with one word.
In response, each team decides on the answer and sends
out those members from its team whose letters are used to
spell the answer. These people line up in correct order
with the first team to correctly answer the question winning the round.

190. WHISK BROOM RELAY

Arrange two teams in parallel lines at one side of the
room. Give the first player of each team a whisk broom
and a six-inch-square sheet of paper. At the signal, he must
stoop to sweep the paper across the room and back, handing
the broom to player number two on his team as soon as he
returns.

Continue until all have taken a turn, with the team finishing first declared winner. This would be an appropriate relay to use in selecting an assistant cleanup committee,
the winning team being excluded from janitorial duties.

191. BALLOON PUSH BALL

Divide the group into two teams and place them at opposite ends of the room. Toss a balloon in the center of the room.

The two teams must race for the balloon, attempting to bat it against the opposing team's wall. The team succeeding in causing the balloon to hit the opposite wall first wins.

A word of warning. Better keep a few extra inflated balloons on hand in case of accidents. If the balloon in play is broken, throw a replacement in at the spot where it happened, without allowing any lag in play.

192. Who's Who Pantomime

For this new game, divide contestants into two teams. Team number one leaves the room, and each player decides on one well-known political, historical, or local leader to portray. Players give a brief pantomime of the personality they represent.

After a designated amount of time, if the character portrayed has not been identified, the player must move to a disqualified line. Play continues until all members of one team have had a chance to perform. The opposite team has a turn, and the team retaining the most players is declared champion.

193. Rhythm

Guests are seated in a line or semicircle for this fast-moving coordination game.

Players number off, with the seats occupied retaining the original number regardless of who moves to sit there. While seated, players are to keep time in unison by hitting first

their knees, then lightly clapping their hands, raising the
right hand with a quick snap as they call out their own
number and snapping two fingers of the left hand as the
number of another player is called.

No number is given except on the snap of the fingers, and
the player's own number must be given first.

Without a break in rhythm, the person whose number
has been called must repeat his number with the first snap
and that of another player on the second. All players keep
up the rhythm motion, with only the players whose numbers are called speaking.

Should any player fail to respond correctly—either by
forgetting his number, failing to answer, or missing the
rhythm—he must move to the foot of the line and all players
with numbers higher than his move down one chair. (Each
player thus acquires a different number to remember.)

Each new round is begun by the player in chair number
one—an honored position which is held as long as possible.
Speed up the action as players become more adept.

194. BIBLE VOCABULARY RHYTHM

Here is a good Bible adaptation of the rhythm game.
Action moves along as outlined for regular rhythm. But on
the first snap, player number one, in beginning the round,
calls out another player's number, and on the second snap,
a proper name from the Bible. The player whose number
was called must go through the rhythm motions and, on
the first finger-snap, call another player's number and then
a Bible word beginning with the last letter in the word just
given.

If, for example, the leader calls out, "five, David," then

number five, keeping in flawless rhythm, must respond with
another player's number and a word such as "Daniel."

The next player could use Leviticus, with the next using
Exodus, etc. As in regular rhythm, failure to keep up the
rhythm, or to respond with an appropriate Bible name,
causes a player to move to the foot of the line.

195. POISON PASS

Seat guests in a circle. As music is played, pass along a
bean bag or any easily handled object around the circle.
When the music stops, the person caught holding the "poison" object must drop out of the game. Play continues until
there is only one player left.

196. WAIST MEASURE

To add a bit of variety to the game schedule, provide
three or four guests with a long piece of string which they
stretch out on the floor. Each player forms the string into
a circle the approximate size of his waist.

Participants then pick up the strings and show each one
how much larger he has made his waist measurement than
it really is.

A clever twist would be to have a few fellows attempt to
estimate the size of their date's waistlines.

197. FOLLOW THE STRING

Lay out a series of strings over and around various ob-

stacles at odd angles. Try to make them all equally difficult. Each contestant is given one end of a string, which
he must wind up as he proceeds over the racing area. With
several players winding and untangling at the same time,
there are certain to be some snags. The first player to successfully wind up all his string is the champion.

198. BALLOON IN THE BASKET

Place a basket in the center of the room, and lay out
four inflated balloons at one side of the room. Give each
contestant a chance to see how long it takes him to kick all
four balloons across the room and into the basket. You
might keep a time limit on each contestant, or perhaps
count the number of kicks necessary to get the balloons
into the basket.

199. BALLOON BURST RELAY

Divide contestants into two or more teams of equal number and give the members of each team a balloon.

At the signal to go, the first contestant on each team begins to blow up his balloon. As soon as it breaks, the next
contestant in line starts blowing his balloon. This continues
on down the line until each player's balloon has been
broken with the team finished first declared winner.

200. RELAY SPELLING BEE

Here is an interesting version of the old and popular

spelldown. Guests are divided into two groups. Take turns giving each group a word to spell. The trick is that each member of a team gives only one letter of the word.

Suppose, for example, the word "encyclopedia" is given. The first person in line, without any prompting from his fellow team members, gives the "e," the next in line the "n," the third the "c" and so on, until the word has been correctly spelled.

If anyone gives an incorrect letter, his team fails to earn a point on that word.

201. STOPWATCH

Here is an interesting contest to use during game time at an adult get-together.

Contestants are to estimate the length of one minute's passing. Someone, acting as referee, uses a watch and, at the signal to begin, contestants attempt to estimate when one minute has passed and call out "stop" when they think this time is over.

202. TEAM SCRAMBLE

This game is best played with a large number of guests and can be used in a number of different settings. Divide players into teams of equal number, and give each team an alphabetical letter so that you have Team A, Team B, Team C, etc.

Blindfold all contestants and scatter them widely throughout the playing area. When the signal to begin has

been given, players move about and attempt to find one
another. No one may speak aloud but must whisper quietly
to the person contacted, asking which team he is from.

If a player locates a member from his team, they move
on together in search of more team members, until the first
team finding all members of its group has been reunited.

203. ONE YARD DASH

This game of skill can be used when individual points
are being accumulated for a prize, or just as an interesting
stunt.

Place a yardstick on the floor with a marble on its surface at one end. Give each contestant a toothpick, and have
them take turns pushing the marble along the length of the
yardstick to the opposite end, without allowing it to roll
off at any point. If it does leave the stick, that contestant
is disqualified or must begin over again.

204. LEVELHEADED RACE

Remind contestants they must keep their heads level to
do well in this race. Give each racer a book of identical
size and weight. At the signal, each contestant balances his
book on top of his head and moves toward a goal line at
the opposite end of the room. He must keep the book balanced at all times. If it falls, he must stop, pick up the
book, and not continue toward the goal until he has taken
his hand away and has the book balanced again.

205. RAISIN FEED

Make up two or more teams of equal number and stand them in single file. Give each team member a tooth pick and a small paper cup containing four raisins.

As the race starts, the first contestant on each team spears the raisins one at a time from his cup and turns to feed the contestant on his team behind him. When the raisins are gone, the second team member turns to feed the next in line, and so on.

Instruct the first contestant to go to the end of the line when he has finished so he can be fed by the last member in line.

206. SEVEN BUZZ

Guests are seated in a line and instructed to begin counting in order. As each player's turn comes, he counts aloud. However, no one may use the number seven in any form. A player, therefore, may not say seven, fourteen, or twenty-one, etc. Instead, when such a number occurs, the contestant must say, "Buzz."

Anyone who fails to use buzz, when it is appropriate, is out of the game. However, if a player makes a mistake and is not discovered before the next person has counted, he may continue in the game.

207. ACTIONS AND ADVERBS

Ask for volunteer couples to try this new game. Couples

take turns going to a specified playing area in front of the
other guests who remain seated.

The boy goes to a hat, and takes out a slip of paper on
which he finds written a common adverb. His partner
draws a slip from another hat on which is written an action to be performed. The girl reads the action and the boy
performs the appropriate action of the adverb.

For example, the action listed might be to turn off the
lights. The adverb drawn by the boy was "wildly." The
boy must then turn off the lights as "wildly" as possible
while the seated players attempt to guess which adverb he
is depicting.

208 SCRAMBLED ALPHABET

Give each player a large supply of alphabet macaroni
or cereal and a short Bible verse which each is to spell out,
using only those letters in his supply. See which contestant
is able to spell out the entire verse first.

To make the game even more exciting, dump all the
alphabet letters in the middle of the table and let guests
dig for the letters they need.

209. HOT POTATO

Players sit in a circle, with one person who is "it" on
his knees in the center. A potato is thrown from guest to
guest around the circle. Since it is a "hot" potato, nobody
may hold it any longer than "it's" count to ten. If anyone
drops the potato and allows "it" to get it, or if "it" intercepts
a player's pass, that person must enter the circle as "it."

210. BACKWARD SPELL DOWN

List a number of common words, not longer than six or eight letters each. Conduct a spell down with each contestant spelling his word backward. When the game has a winner, award that person a prize as the most backward guest at the party.

211. RING PASS

Divide players into two equal groups and line them up facing each other. Give each contestant a toothpick to put in his mouth. The leader starts a ring down the line on each side, which must be passed along by slipping it from one player's toothpick, held between his teeth, to that of the next player, without using the hands at any time.

Should the ring drop, it must be returned to the player at the head of the line on its way down, or at the foot of the line on its way back.

212. WHO IS THAT TV PERSONALITY?

Five or six guests are selected from the group and each given a slip of paper with the name of a well-known television personality. Be sure to use people who are unique in the way they appear on the TV screen.

Each participant takes a turn standing up to attempt an imitation of the personality named on his slip of paper. Award a prize to the guest doing the best job of impersonation. Decisions can be based on how quickly the person is correctly guessed.

PART FOUR

∴

WEAR YOUR OLD CLOTHES, KIDS

Children love games. And the fresh air and wide open space of an outdoor playing area seem to act as an extra incentive to youngster's enthusiasm for fun.

Recognizing the fact that children enjoy playacting, many of the games in this section require roles as animals, storybook characters and grown-up occupations.

Be sure the players are appropriately dressed. Schedule rest periods between active games, and encourage a sense of participation with good sportsmanship.

You may very well discover yourself having as much fun as the kids!

213. GRAY WOLF

If the group is not large and an outdoor playing area
is available, introduce the game of gray wolf.

One player is chosen to be the gray wolf. Everyone else
is a sheep. All the sheep have a fold, where they are safe
from the wolf. The wolf has a den. When a sheep has been
caught, it is placed in the wolf's den, and cannot be freed
until a fellow sheep runs to the den and touches his hand.

If the rescuer can get there safely, the two are allowed
to return to the sheepfold. If the wolf is successful in
capturing all the sheep, or if too much time passes before
he can catch everyone, a new gray wolf is chosen.

214. CIRCLE THE SUN

Here is a new game for children to play at a picnic or
other outdoor activity. Contestants are divided into two
teams and situated on two goals some distance apart. Team
number one begins the game as astronauts. The opposite
team members are meteorites. The object of the game is for
the astronauts to race toward the meteor's goal, representing the sun, and then return to their own goal, earth.

They make their way to the sun and back, moving from
safety zone to safety zone. Zones are marked off as planets.
As long as a runner is on a planet, he cannot be hit by a
meteorite. When a player is tagged, however, he must aid
the meteorites in their pursuit.

If an astronaut will not leave the safety of a planet, all
of the meteorites can get behind that planet and count to
ten. The runner must leave for the next safety zone or
join the meteorites.

215. Poor Lame Fox

Begin the game by choosing one player to act as the lame fox. He stands at a goal while the other players move toward him, teasing and taunting.

When the fox decides to chase the players, he may take three giant steps. After taking these first three steps, he must hop on one foot the rest of the way to the safety zone.

If he catches anyone, that person becomes his helper, and they continue chasing the other players in the manner described until everyone has been caught.

216. Goal

Players are arranged in a circle, standing with their legs spaced wide apart. One player stands in the center with either a volleyball or a basketball. He tries to score by rolling the ball between the outstretched legs of one of the players in the circle.

A player may only stop the ball with his hands. He must not bring his legs together. In addition, hands must be kept on hips, except when a ball is coming toward him. When the center player scores a goal, he and the player who allowed the ball to pass change places.

217. Carry the Water

Divide contestants into pairs for this race and give each couple a sheet of newspaper the same size and a glass of water. When the signal is given, the water must be carefully poured on the newspaper without spilling any.

Teams begin racing forward together, each pair holding an end of the newspaper. Partners may keep going as long as the water has not soaked through to make a hole in the paper. When this does happen, the team must immediately stop.

The team able to cover the farthest distance is declared winner.

218. Ring Around the Peg

Push a long pencil into the ground and give each contestant eight rubber rings to toss from a distance of a few feet away. The one who gets the most rings onto the pencil is the winner. A box of pencils would be an appropriate prize.

219. Stepping Stones

Here is a new game to be played outdoors. Mark off circles on the dirt, or with chalk if the game is played on a cement surface. Begin the game by placing a stone large enough to be seen inside each marked out circle.

Players may move from one circle to another as long as the game leader is clapping both hands. However, when the leader blows a whistle, players scurry to stand on a circle. There will not be enough circles for all the players, and as only one player is allowed on each circle, some will be eliminated.

The leader then begins to remove one stone after each

round so that players must search for only those circle areas with stones on them. Any other circle does not count.

220. BEWARE THE WATER SPRITE

This old game comes from China. It is based on a super-stition among the Chinese that, after a hard rain or thaw when there is fresh water flowing down a stream, a water sprite waits in the middle of the stream, hoping to bewitch anyone who tries to cross.

Players are divided into two groups, with one group standing on one side of a marked off area representing the stream, the other on the opposite side. One player acts the role of the water sprite and stands in the stream.

The water sprite beckons to any member he choses of either group. That person, in turn, beckons to a player standing on the opposite side. These two switch sides by running across the stream, trying as they run to avoid being tagged by the water sprite. If one player is touched by the sprite, he must change places with him, as the game continues.

221. OBSTACLE COURSE

This is an exciting game for children and is especially suitable for rural areas and picnics.

Gather a pile of tree limbs and lay out a path-like pattern. Use two contestants, sending them blindfolded, one at one end and the other at the opposite end, to see how long it takes them to get together. Warn them they are not to step over a log or they will be returned to the right place. The two contestants are allowed to assist each other by calling out instructions.

222. Freeze Tag

Stand players in a circle, with someone chosen as "it" placed in the center, holding a large soft ball or bean bag. Mark off a boundary area for the game, and instruct players to keep all game activity within this boundary.

"It" tosses the ball high into the air and the other players begin to scatter quickly within the marked boundaries. As soon as "it" catches the ball, he calls out "freeze." Every player must stop in his tracks and stand still while "it" tries to hit someone with the ball.

If he does, the person hit becomes "it" for the next game. If "it" fails to hit anyone (any person hit on the legs or feet while the ball is rolling also is considered tagged), the game is continued with everyone running while he retrieves the ball. As soon as he picks it up and calls "freeze" again, players stop, and he tries to score a hit.

223. Fence Tag

If there is a low, wooden fence or hedge in the playing area, (or you may simply mark a line), stage a game of tag with "it" on one side and the players on the other. Whenever a player jumps over the fence, he can be chased by "it." To get back to safety and avoid being tagged, he jumps to the safe side of the fence. If tagged, of course, he must be "it" and the game continues.

224. SNOWMAN TAG

This game is played just like regular tag, except that, to be safe, a player must freeze in position like a snowman, no matter how awkward this may be. If he is moving any part of his body when "it" touches him, then he and "it" change places.

225. SQUIRREL TAG

This is a good tag game to be played in an area where there are a lot of trees with low limbs. Someone is chosen to be the squirrel hunter, while the other players act as squirrels.

The hunter chases the squirrels around the playing area, and the only way a squirrel is safe is to hang from a tree. Whenever a squirrel is tagged, he becomes the new hunter.

226. BACK TO BACK SAFETY TAG

A different variation on the old game of tag is to allow players to be free from tagging when they have positioned themselves back to back with another player.

227. WOOD TAG

Mark out boundaries and confine this game of tag to a specific area. A player is safe from being tagged by "it" as long as some part of his body is touching an object made of wood. This could be a tree, bush, stump, fence post, etc. Metal or stone could also be used in place of wood.

228. Toe Twins

Play this tag game like any other, except that a player can not be tagged as long as the toe of one of his shoes is touching the toe of another player's shoe.

229. Rainy Day

Players are situated along a goal line, which is a safe shelter from the "rain."

Someone starts as a lone raindrop, standing several yards away from the other players. The game leader acts as a weatherman, and stands with an umbrella in his hands. If an umbrella is not available, the weatherman can raise both arms as a signal that it has begun to rain.

As long as he keeps the umbrella down, it is a sunny day and the players are safe in leaving the shelter area. However, they do not leave until the weatherman tells them the weather is fine.

They move toward the raindrop until the weatherman opens his umbrella or raises both arms calling, "It's a rainy day." This is the signal for the raindrop to race toward the players in an attempt to catch one. The person caught is also a raindrop and must help next time.

This continues, with the raindrops increasing in number until every player has been properly "drenched."

230. GUARD THE CASTLE

One player is selected to be king and marks off a small area to represent his castle. The other players come up to the "walls" of the castle and tease the king by stepping inside. The king tries to catch them inside the castle. They are safe outside the boundary line, but anyone caught inside becomes the king, and the former king joins the players outside the castle.

231 CAT AND MICE

Appoint one player to be the cat, designating the rest of the players as mice.

A tree is chosen to be the cat's nest, and the cat waits beside it, while the mice gather around to tease him. The cat is not allowed to chase a mouse, until one of them has been bold enough to scratch somewhere on the tree.

As soon as the cat hears a mouse scratch, he chases him. If he can catch this mouse before it gets back to the safety of the nest, then that mouse becomes a cat, too, and helps catch more mice.

232. DOG ON HIS LEASH

Tie a length of rope to a post or tree in the center of the playing area. One player is the dog and holds one end of the rope. The other contestants move close to tantalize him.

The dog can chase these players anytime he wishes but

cannot go any farther than to the end of the rope. When
he catches a player, the two change places.

233. CIRCLE BALL KEEPAWAY

Players form a circle, with a leader in the center. One
player in the circle holds a large ball. When the leader
calls "go," the player must begin throwing the ball to
other players in the circle, while the leader tries to inter-
cept. When he does catch the ball, the player last to
throw it takes his place in the center.

234. BUMPING

This outdoor game will be especially enjoyed by boys.
Players are paired off with one pair designated to do
the bumping. Each boy lifts up his left knee and holds it
against his stomach, using both arms. When the signal is
given, players hop toward each other and charge with their
shoulders in an attempt to knock each other off balance.

When a contestant's lifted foot touches the ground, or
one arm is unfolded, that player must leave and a new
player takes his place.

The game can be made a tournament by eliminating
players who were bumped out in the first round, and
matching winners.

235. SOMERSAULT RACE

Here is another game especially for the boys.

Line up the contestants, and at the signal to begin, each moves toward the opposite goal by turning a forward somersault. No walking or crawling is allowed.

236. HIDE AND SEEK

This favorite old game is well adaptable to a wide variety of playing areas. It can be played in the house or outside, as long as there are good hiding places available.

Someone is chosen to be "it," and stands at a base, hiding his eyes as he counts to one hundred. As he is counting, the other players run to find hiding places within predetermined boundaries.

When "it" reaches one hundred, he calls out, "Here I come, ready or not."

If any player can sneak out of his hiding place and get back to the base before "it" can catch him, he has come in free and will not be "it" for the next game. As soon as "it" locates a hidden player, he runs back to the base, stamps on it twice an calls the person's name.

The first person thus found will be "it" for the next game.

237. SPOTLIGHT HIDE AND SEEK

This game must be played at night in an area with a good variety of hiding places. Play it the same way as regular hide and seek, except that "it" carries a flashlight to spot out the hidden players.

As soon as a player is caught in the beam of light, that one must go to the base. Play continues until everyone has been caught. The first one spotlighted is "it."

238. GRAB THE AMMUNITION

Mark off a line through the center of the playing area. In the middle of each divided zone, place a pile of six sticks, representing ammunition. Then off in one corner of each side, mark out a prison area. Players are divided into two teams and scattered around their war zones.

The point of the game is to cross the goal line and grab a stick of ammunition without being caught by the other side. As soon as a player has crossed the boundary line, he can be caught by the players from the "enemy team" and put into their prison. When a player is in prison, he can only be released when one of his teammates runs across the border to touch his hand. If they can make contact before the rescuer is caught, the two may return safely behind their lines. If a player does get to the ammunition pile and grabs a stick, he is safe as long as he stands there holding it. If he decides to run with it, however, he is vulnerable to attack and may be put into prison with the ammunition stick returned.

Or, he can choose to wait until a team member runs to the stick pile and is also successful in grabbing another stick. Then the two may return safely to their own side. When one team has stolen all the ammunition from the opposite side's pile, they have won the battle.

239. WEAKEST LINK

This is a good game for younger boys blessed with a

plentiful supply of energy. Have them join hands to form a
circle. At a signal to begin, each boy moves out farther
and farther, making the circle grow, until someone is forced
to release his hold. Then he and the person's hand he was
holding when the break occurred must leave the circle
while the game continues.

240. FUGITIVES

Players choose sides to form two teams. Give team number one a supply of white sheets of paper. Allow a five
minute start and tell the leader of team one that a sheet of
paper must be attached every few yards to objects along
the trail. After five minutes team number two sets out to
chase the fugitives. The fugitive team circles at a given
point and moves back to the starting line. If group one
gets back safely, it is the winner. If group number two
catches up with them, the fugitives lose the contest.

241. BOY-GIRL TUG OF WAR

The boys pull from one side and the girls from the other.
The only difference in this tug of war is that the girls may
use both hands to pull, but the boys are only allowed the
use of one hand.

242. STATUE

Line up players at a starting line, facing an opposite

goal about thirty yards away. A leader stands halfway
between the two goals and, with his eyes covered, begins
counting to ten. As he counts, all the players move forward toward the opposite goal.

As soon as he reaches ten, the leader calls out "statue."
When he says this, everyone must freeze into the position
held when the word was called out. If the leader catches
any player moving after "statue" has been called, that player
must go back to the beginning line.

As the runners reach the opposite goal, they turn around
and come back toward the beginning goal. If a player is
caught moving on the return trip, he goes back to the last
goal touched.

The first player to complete both trips is the winner and
acts as leader for the next game.

243. To Market, To Market

Tell players they are to be real pigs in this game and
allow them to grunt and carry on in true pig fashion, as
they line up on a goal line for the game to begin.

One player stands about twenty or thirty yards away,
acting as the market man. As the pigs leave their goal, they
chant the first line of the well-known nursery rhyme, "to
market, to market, to buy a fat pig." They chant this very
slowly and must move forward to just within a few feet
of the market man.

When he decides to do so, the market man answers,
"home again, home again, jiggidy-jig." When he finishes
saying this, the pigs race back to their goal and the market
man tries to capture one of them. If he does, that pig

becomes another market man and the two attempt to catch more pigs in the next round.

Play continues until all the pigs have been caught.

244. MUSICAL MATS

This version of musical chairs is adaptable to outside play if a recorder or other source of music is available there.

Place several pieces of cardboard, representing bases, around the yard, and as music is played, guests mill about. When the music stops, each scurries to find a base. As there is always one less base than players, a contestant is eliminated each time.

Play continues until only one player remains.

245. SQUAT TAG

This is an old favorite among children and is simple to play anywhere, however, keep the action confined to within a specified area.

Someone is chosen to be "it," and chase the other players. If "it" can tag anyone who is standing upright, that player must assume the duties of chaser. However, players are safe if they squat before "it" has touched them.

246. HANDICAPPED TAG

Play this game like regular tag, with a person as "it" standing between two goal lines. "It" is blindfolded and tries to tag players as they move past him from one safety goal to another. The players must move with their feet in burlap bags. They are not blindfolded but attempt to creep as quietly as possible past "it" to keep from being tagged.

As soon as a player is tagged, he climbs out of his bag and is blindfolded to help catch the others.

247. NO ARMS TAG

Players including "it" must keep their hands tightly clasped behind their backs at all times. "It" must tag a player by brushing against him.

248. ONE -ARMED KEEP AWAY

An interesting variation of the old favorite, "one-armed keep away" is played in the usual manner, except that each contestant must keep one arm tightly folded behind him at all times, using only one arm to toss the ball among his team members. Anyone using both arms will cause his team to forfeit the ball to the other side.

249. HOME BASE

Players are divided into two teams, each positioned on a goal line with a "no man's land" of thirty yards or so between. All of the players from one team come out to challenge the players of the other. They are then open for chase, as the last team to touch its base is the one who does the pursuing.

Players move close to the other goal to tease someone to run off the base. If he chases anyone from the opposite team, and that player gets safely back to his own base, he can then turn around and chase that player.

When a player is caught, he is taken back to the opposite goal. Whoever has caught him may not be captured while he is escorting a player to the goal. One section of the home base is marked off as a prison for the captured players. These players stand with arms outstretched, waiting for team mates to get them free. If anyone from the opposite team gets to the prison safely, he can free a team mate and return to his home base without being captured. Each side tries to catch all the members of the opposite team.

250. What Time Is It, Mr. Fox?

One player acts as the fox, standing some distance from the other players with his back to them. Players advance from a safety zone, chanting, "What time is it, Mr. Fox?"

The fox answers any time of the day except midnight. Players wait for his answer before advancing another few steps, as they repeat, "What time is it, Mr. Fox?" When the fox decides to call, "Midnight," he quickly turns and chases the players, tagging as many as possible before they can return to the safety of the goal line. All tagged must act as the fox's assistants in capturing the rest.

251. Dodge the Satellite.

Attach a bean bag to the end of a long rope. Players

stand in a wide circle with the leader in the center. The
game leader swings the bag at the end of the rope, keeping
it a few inches from the floor.

Players must jump over the rope as it comes around to
their feet. If the rope or satellite hits a player, he must
leave the circle. As the players become fewer in number,
the game leader may swing th rope faster and higher.

252. RED BUTTON

Mark off two parallel lines about forty feet apart. Position
all players behind these lines. In the middle territory,
place one player who is "it."

"It" calls out three times, "Red Button, Red Button, Red
Button." When he has said this the third time, all players
rush across to the opposite side, chased by the center
player. Anyone he catches helps from then on in chasing
the others.

"It" may chose to trick or tantalize the runners by
saying, "Green Button, Blue Button," etc. Any player
starting across at the wrong signal is automatically captured
and joins the others in the center. This is also true for
those players who begin running before the third "Red
Button" has been called.

Still another way to fool the runners is for one of the
captured players other than "it" to call out Red Button.

The first player caught is "it" for the next game.

253. SCARED RABBIT

Players are divided into groups of three and scattered

about the playground. Two of the three form a "nest," by facing each other and clasping hands. The third acts as the rabbit and waits in his house.

There must be two extra players—a homeless rabbit and a hunter. The hunter begins the game by chasing the homeless rabbit in and out around the group. When the rabbit becomes tired, he may enter one of the nests and, immediately, the rabbit who was hiding there must leave to be chased by the hunter. When the hunter catches a rabbit, they change roles.

254. KICK THE CAN

Here is an exciting twist to the old children's favorite hide and seek game.

Select a goal and place a tin can next to "it." Someone who is chosen to be "it" hides his eyes while he counts aloud to fifty. All the other players scamper to find hiding places.

At the end of the count, "it" begins his search. When he locates a hiding player, they race back to the goal.

If "it" tags the goal before the other player is able to, he has a prisoner who must wait near the goal as "it" goes off to hunt again. While "it" is gone, a comrade player may sneak out of hiding to free one prisoner by kicking the can beside the goal and yelling, "prisoner go free."

The freed prisoner and player who assisted him go to find new hiding places.

"It" must continue hunting until he has made all the players prisoner. The first player to have been caught is "it" for the next round. However, this is a game that can last quite some time if the players are especially crafty.

255. BLIND MAN'S BLUFF

Blind man's bluff is one of the oldest games recorded and is played by children all over the world.

One player is blindfolded and stands in the center, as the others join hands and begin circling around him. When the blind man claps his hands three times, the circle halts while the blind man points toward one of the players. Whichever player is pointed out must step into the circle, where he is chased by the blind man.

When the player has been caught, the blind man attempts to guess the player's identity. If he does so correctly, they change places. If not, the captured player returns to the circle, and the game continues.

The chosen player may try by various means to slip quietly around the circle. However, when he has been caught, he must wait while the blind man attempts to identify him.

256. ANIMAL BLIND MAN'S BLUFF

One blindfolded player stands holding a long stick in the center of the circle. While the rest of the players skip around him in a circle, he begins tapping three times on the floor with his stick. After he taps the third time, everyone stand still. The blind man points his stick at one of the players, who moves into the circle to take the opposite end of the stick in his hand.

The blind man orders the other player to imitate an animal noise, such as a cow, lion, duck or dog would make. From this sound, the blind man attempts to guess the name of the player. If he can guess correctly, the two switch places. But if he is wrong, the game is repeated, using the same blind man.

257. WHO KICKED THE BUCKET?

Line up players in a semicircle, facing an empty bucket. "It" stands with his back to the bucket while someone from the circle steps out and kicks the bucket. He is accompanied by two or three others players, who pretend by the motion of their feet and facial expression that they were the kickers.

"It" turns around and attempts to guess who did it. If successful, he changes places with the kicker. Otherwise, he turns and the game continues.

258. BLINDFOLD RELAY RACE

Before the race begins, divide the contestants into two teams of equal and even numbers. Divide each team in half again and number members so there are two ones, two two's two threes, etc. Stand half of each team at one goal line, the other half at the opposite goal in single file.

Give each team a letter of the alphabet.

To begin the contest, the first runner from Team A starts out, blindfolded, across the racing area toward the goal on the opposite end. As he moves forward, he calls out his team's letter, followed by his own number. He may say, "A-1, A-1, A-1."

The member of the opposite half of his team with the same number, who is also blindfolded, calls out in response. As soon as the runner is able to locate and touch the hand

of that contestant, he can remove his blind, and his teammate makes his way blindfolded toward the opposite goal.

No coaching may be given by those who have completed
the race and removed their blindfolds.

259. MYSTERY ANIMALS

Divide players into two teams and place them on goals
about fifty yards apart. One of the teams begins the activity
by secretly choosing the name of some animal whose
sound can be imitated. The team proceeds together toward
the other goal and, as it comes within a few yards, the
members of the opposite team, following their leader, begin
making one animal sound after another until they guess
the sound of the animal that has been chosen.

When they guess correctly, the animals rush back to
their goal pursued by the opposite team. Any players captured become members of the opposite team.

As soon as the animals reach their goal, members of the
opposite team become animals, selecting a new species.

260. SPIDER AND THE FLY

Choose one player to begin the game as the spider, and
place him in a circle marked off on the ground about ten
feet in diameter. This will be the spider's web.

The spider must wait here, while the other contestants,
acting out the role of flies, come up toward him.

The flies tease the spider, using both feet, until they
reach the boundaries of the web. If they wish, they may
move closer to the spider, but they must hop on one foot.

If chased by the spider, a fly must still hop on one foot until he gets out of the web.

The spider may use both feet at all times but is restricted within his web. When any fly is captured, he becomes a new spider and the old spider becomes a fly.

261. Moon and Morning Stars

Explain to the group that this is a game enjoyed by little Spanish children. It must be played when there is a bright sun overhead so the player who is the moon may find a large shaded area near an open, sunny one. All other players are called morning stars and move toward the moon's shaded spot to tease him.

The moon ignores their taunts but waits for an opportunity to catch one of the stars before that star can get safely back into the sunlight. When this happens, the moon and captured star change places.

262. Capture the Bear

Players join hands in a circle, forming a bear-pit with one player as the bear in the middle. The object of the game is for the bear to make frantic attempts to escape his pit by breaking apart the clapsed hands in the circle, or going over or under them.

If he is successful, all the other players chase him, with the player first catching him becoming the next bear.

The bear can throw his prisoners off guard by such tactics as seeming to break through at one spot, then suddenly turning to crawl under another.

263. Serpent's Tail

Guests stand in a circle, with four or five players in the center. These players form the "serpent" by standing in single file with their hands on the shoulders of the player in front of them.

A beach ball is tossed about the circle until an opportunity arises to strike the "tail" of the serpent—the player at the end of the center line.

The player striking a blow goes to the head of the serpent line and the player struck joins the circle. The serpent squirms and races around the circle in an attempt to keep from being struck.

264. Double Catch

This is an especially good game for handicapped players who may have difficulty catching a thrown object.

Divide players into two teams, each placed on its own goal line facing one another, with a no man's land of about sixty feet between them.

A referee stands in the center, holding a volleyball or basketball. When he gives a signal, each team proceeds cautiously out to the center. When the teams are both quite close to him, the referee points to one team—he will alternate between the two as the game continues—and throws the ball high into the air.

One of the members of the team he has pointed out must catch the ball. If he succeeds, all the members of that team pursue the members of the opposite team who have been waiting for the catch. If the ball is not caught, then the opposite team does the chasing.

265. Rocket Race

Provide each contestant with an oblong balloon. At the go signal, each begins to bat his "rocket" toward the goal line. The first one there is the winner.

If a balloon falls out of orbit, it can be picked up. However, if it is carried or bursts, the contestant is disqualified from the race.

266. Name Your Trade

Divide players into two teams and assign each team a goal line. The teams stand on their goal lines, facing each other.

One team begins the game by marching up to the other and calling, "Here we come." Members of the opposite team ask, "Where from?" The approaching team answers, "From Kalamazoo." The question is then asked, "Name your trade." The answer comes back, "Lemonade." Then the waiting team questions, "How is it made?"

After this last question has been asked, the approaching players begin acting out a trade they had previously decided on. It could be washing clothes, picking cotton, bricklaying, or any of a number of trades with actions to be pantomined.

As soon as any member of the other team correctly guesses the trade, all the members of the team acting it out must turn and race back to the safety of their goal line. Any who are caught become members of the opposite team.

267. MERRILY GO ROUND

Have guests join hands to form a circle. One player is "it," and walks around the outside of the circle a few times before striking the joined hands of two players.

These two immediately begin running, one to the left and the other to the right. "It" steps into the gap and the first runner back fills the other empty spot. The second runner back is "it" for the next round.

268. HANSEL AND GRETEL

This game is adapted from the well-known classic and can best be played in a small wooded area or among shrubs.

Someone is chosen to begin the game as the witch, who locates her house in the woods. She remains in her house while the other children make their way from tree to tree.

As they approach, she sits motionless until they are close enough to chase. Suddenly, she leaps up and runs after them, tagging as many as she can before they get back to the safety area. Any player tagged must drop to the ground and wait there. The witch collects these children on her way back to her house. There the children are "baked" into gingerbread and placed in a cupboard where they must wait without trying to escape. Meanwhile, all the children who escaped return to the woods. This time they try to tease the witch to chase them away from her house, so some of the free players can slip back to the cupboard. Anyone who makes it there safely, touches the hand of one gingerbread child and the two get away free. But anyone caught by the witch while trying to free a player is also baked into gingerbread.

269. SIAMESE TAG

Number off players by twos and form couples of the ones and twos. These groups must hold hands throughout the game.

Tag is played under regular rules, except that couples do the tagging together. One member of the "it" couple may tag any member of another group. It isn't necessary for both members of the "it team" to touch the other couple at the same time. Mark off a safety zone for tired twins.

270. HOOK-ON TAG

Divide players into groups of three and line up each group in a file three deep, with numbers two and three holding an arm around the waist of the player in front of them.

One player acts as the chaser and tries to attach himself in the same manner to the rear player of any group he can catch. When he succeeds, the head of the threesome must unhook and become the new chaser.

Groups attempt by switching and dodging to keep facing the chaser and prevent his attaching himself to their end.

271. BOX TAG

Play this game like ordinary tag, except the person who is "it" carries a large cardboard box. He must attempt to place the box over the head of a player. Once "boxed," the runner is automatically "it."

Players cannot force the box with their hands, and the box need not remain on someone's head for that person to be "it."

272. EAST AND WEST TAG

Guests are grouped around the playing area in couples, standing back to back with one player facing east and the other west. A lone player is "it." He walks around the group and calls out either east or west. The player facing the direction he calls must change places with someone else, while "it" tries to get a partner. If "it" succeeds, the player left without a partner becomes the new "it."

273. CAT AND RAT

This game is a great favorite with young children and is not too rough for both boys and girls to play together.

Choose one player to start the game as a cat and another as the rat. Remaining players form a circle by clasping hands. The cat waits outside the circle, with the rat standing inside.

As the game begins, there is a banter between cat and rat.

The cat calls out, "I am the cat."

The rat says, "I am the rat."

The cat says, "I will catch you."

The rat responds, "You can't."

This last statement is the signal for a chase to begin. The cat must try to enter the circle, while the rat attempts to keep away from him. Both may run in and out of the circle, but players assist the rat by opening their arms for him, while blocking the progress of the chasing cat.

When the rat has been caught, he joins the circle. The cat becomes a rat, with a new cat being chosen.

274. CIRCLE DODGE BALL

Divide players into two equally numbered groups. One group forms a loose circle and the other players stand inside. The ring of players toss a large, soft ball at the players inside.

Whenever one is hit on the legs or feet, he must leave the center of the circle. This keeps on until only one player remains in the middle and is declared champion.

275. HANDKERCHIEF GRAB

Players are divided into teams with each team counting off consecutively. The number one player from each team comes out, with one of them carrying a handkerchief, which he holds teasingly in front of the other player, who must try to grab it and race back to his team without being caught.

If he does so, he earns a point for his team. But if he is caught before he can get back, the opposite team gets the point. When the handkerchief has been returned, the number one player return to the center and the action is repeated, with the other player holding the handkerchief. This continues until each member of each team has had a turn to hold and to grab the handkerchief.

276. Gwendolyn and Marmaduke

Form players in a circle, and select a boy and girl to stand in the center ring. The boy is called Marmaduke, the girl is Gwendolyn.

Blindfold only the girl. Gwendolyn must attempt to locate Marmaduke by calling out his name and listening for his answer. Whenever she calls, "Marmaduke," he must call back, "Gwendolyn." When the boy has been caught, another couple take their place.

277. Mysterious Mr. It

Assemble contestants in an area designated as the goal. Have them turn their backs and close their eyes with their hands extended behind them. As they do, the game leader places a small object into one player's hand. He is careful in doing so that no other member of the group knows who has the object.

Then players are instructed to close their hands, turn around and open their eyes. Players move out into the playing area, with the one who is holding the small object trying to keep it a secret. After a few minutes, the leader calls, "Beware of Mr. It."

The person who has the object then calls, "I'm Mr. It," and begins chasing the other players, tagging as many as he can before they get back to the safety of the goal. Those players tagged are eliminated from the game, while Mr. "It" takes a turn placing the object into some other player's hand in the same manner as before.

278. MOUNTAIN GOATS

This game can best be played in an area where there is
a good collection of large rocks, fallen logs, or both. However, crates or chairs can also be used.

One player is chosen to be the lion. All other players are
mountain goats. The goats are chased about the playing
area by the mountain lion and can escape only by leaping
up off the ground to perch on a rock or log.

The lion is not allowed to tag a goat unless it is running
from one object over to another. However, only one goat
may ccupy a perch at one time. If one goat jumps up on a
safe place, the goat already there must immediately leave
and be chased by the lion.

Whenever any goat is tagged, he becomes a lion.

279. WILD ANIMAL HUNT

Children love games in which they can pretend to be
animals.

Appoint one player to act as the hunter, while all the
others are to be animals. The animals count off by fours,
and a different jungle animal is assigned to each. The ones
might be lions, the twos, tigers, the threes, elephants, and
the fours, monkeys. Give the hunter a soft ball or bean bag
for his ammunition.

All the animals are lined up facing an opposite goal line,
with the hunter standing between.

The hunter calls out the names of any of the four animals
he wishes. If he calls "lions," all the lions must try to run
across to the opposite goal line. As they run, the hunter

attempts to "down" one of them with his ball. Any animal
hit changes places to become the new hunter.

For variety, the hunter may call, "The jungle is burning."
When he says this, all of the animals must race across to
the opposite goal line.

280. BATTLE OF THE KNIGHTS

This is a rough and tumble game that will appeal to boys.
Contestants are divided into teams with two on a team.
One is the horse and the other the knight. When the signal
is given, the riders jump on the backs of their horses, arms
and legs wrapped around them. The point of the contest
is that each rider attempts to knock the other knights off
their horses, while remaining fixed on his own mount.

281. JUMBLE UP

Most children are adventurous enough to join heartily in
the spirit of each game suggested. However, if at some
point the game comes to a standstill and players are re-
luctant to leave their safety zones to be chased or venture
from a goal toward the person acting as "it," the game
leader may choose to call out, "Jumble up," and each player
must make some move from his spot to get the game back
into action.

282. BIRD WATCHER'S HIKE

If the children are not familiar with the native birds of

your area, you will want to study together from an illustrated book several days before the hike is scheduled. The best time for bird watching is just as dawn begins to break. Caution the hikers to remain as quiet as possible and be sure to instruct as many as possible to bring along a pair of field glasses. Make a game of the number of different birds identified.

283. CONCENTRATION HIKE

Hike a group of children through an area that includes a good variety of objects. Give each child instructions to make careful note of everything he sees along the way. When the hike is finished, give each hiker a pencil and paper with instructions to list the different objects seen.

284. STARLIGHT HIKE

Before the hike, be sure to note some astronomical facts, as well as some related Scriptural references. The evening's program could include some information on great astronomers in history as well as some twentieth century facts on the space program.

285. LISTEN

During one of the rest stops on a hike, instruct everyone to sit absolutely still for five minutes. Give each a pencil and paper with instructions to list all the different sounds heard and to identify them.

286. Nature Quiz

When you return from a nature hike on which you have
given out a great deal of facts and illustrations, conduct a
written quiz to see which hiker can recall the most information learned during the hike.

287. Snowball Tag Game

In this game, only "it" is allowed to throw snowballs.
Instruct him to take care that they are soft enough to prevent injury. Any player hit by one of the snowballs becomes "it."

288. Circle Tag

Mark out a large circle in the snow and have contestants
number off.

One by one, they run into the circle area when their
number is called by the game leader. When he hears his
number, each player begins running forward, following the
circle and trying to keep away from the runner behind him.
Each runner tries to tag the shoulder of the runner in front
of him, eliminating that runner from competition.

At any point, however, the game leader may call, "Reverse." When this happens, all runners turn to chase the
person behind them, keeping away from the runner they
were just chasing.

289. SHERIFF AND OUTLAWS

Here is a winter game that children will enjoy for hours on end.

Lay out a network of snow trails leading to and from the outlaw's den. One player is chosen to be sheriff. The others are outlaws. Players must stay on the trails at all times.

When an outlaw is tagged, he is brought to the jail to wait until another prisoner comes. As soon as there are two prisoners in jail, another outlaw can set free the one who got there first. He does this by touching his hand.

290. MUSH

If you have sleds available at an ice skating party, divide contestants into teams of two. One skates, pulling a sled, while his partner rides along, driving the "team."

291. ESKIMO TUG OF WAR

Have contestants build a wall of snow with a large hole in the center. When you are ready to begin, put a rope through the hole and have the two tug of war teams take their positions. The team which is pulled against the wall, causing it to collapse, loses.

292. HATS OFF THE SNOWMAN

Build a large snowman and place a hat on his head. Con-

testants pile up a supply of snowballs and, standing thirty
yards away, each is given six throws to try to knock off the
snowman's hat.

293. SLED HOCKEY

This is a winter game that will especially appeal to the
boys. Have each boy bring his own sled. Provide him with
two long spikes, which he uses to propel his sled around
on the ice.

Use a basketball for the hockey puck and conduct the
game just like regular ice hockey.

Contestants are not allowed to get off their sleds. They
move about by stabbing into the ice to pull forward. The
ball may not be touched by hand, but only butted with a
contestant's sled.

294. TRACK DOWN

Boys are especially fond of this intriguing game, which is
played in an area covered by freshly fallen snow. Three
or four contestants act as the fugitives and are allowed
about five minute's head start. The others form a posse and
set out to find their trail.

295. FOX AND GEESE

Here is an old favorite to play in a large area covered by
snow that has not been marred by tracks. Mark out a play-

ing area by shuffling a circular path in the snow, criss-crossed by paths cutting through the center.

One player acts as the fox and the rest of the group are geese. The center of the circle is the safety zone for all geese. The fox may pass through the center in pursuit of a goose but may not tag anyone resting there. Anyone the fox tags is the new fox and the old fox joins the geese.

296. COASTING SKATE RACE

If there will be ice skating included in the party activity, conduct a coasting race. Mark off a starting line where contestants must begin coasting. Allow each skater an area to get underway, then keep record of the one coasting the farthest distance from the starting point.

297. RACE THE SNOWBALL

Conduct this contest on a day when the snow is soft and easily packed.

Roll one snowball of equal size for each team and line up contestants at the starting line. As a signal is given, each team begins rolling its snowball toward a goal area. As the snowballs become larger, they will be more difficult to move.

The winner will be determined by the size of the ball as well as which team arrived first to the finishing line. Use some of the best balls to assemble a snowman, if you like.

Perhaps you might want to combine two or three teams, having members work together for a prize-winning snow statue.

298. Retrieve the Arrow

Divide contestants into two teams and have team members number off by twos. Ones stand at a certain point; the twos at another. Give the ones on each team a bow and arrow. The ones act as archers and the twos will retrieve for them.

When the signal is given, the first archer for each team shoots an arrow as far as he can. (Mark the arrows carefully so they can be easily identified.) A runner from the ones retrieves an arrow shot by his team member and vice versa.

The first one back wins a point for his side. When the runner gets back, the arrows are given to the second archers, while the next runner prepares to go out and get them.

299. Ice Cream Licking Contest

Dip a large scoop of ice cream into a dish for each guest. Contestants stand with hands behind their backs and, when the signal is given, begin licking the ice cream. Keep a close watch to be sure they do not use their teeth. The first one to clean his dish is the winner.

300. Clean up Contest

After a children's picnic or party outside, plan a final game in which you award an attractive prize to the guest who can collect the biggest pile of debris scattered about the area. You'll be setting a good example for the children and will leave the area cleaner than when you arrived.

PART FIVE

●
●
●

PLEASE DON'T WALK ON THE PIANO

Children's indoor parties require a good choice of games in order to be successful. The game leader needs a firm touch to keep activities under control, as well as an enthusiastic approach to game time.

For very young children, keep the games simple and uncomplicated by elaborate rules and procedures. A valuable aid in establishing recreational rapport with young players is sensing the best time to switch to a new game. This should be done when interest is at a high pitch.

When games are included in the activities of a birthday party or holiday celebration, with definite starting and ending times, plan a series of quiet games before the children leave to help calm and rest them. Be sure to move breakable objects safely from the playing area, and if you must tell young guests not to walk on the piano, smile when you say it!

301. TOWER RACE

Teams line up behind two towers built by piling up checkers or blocks. Each tower should contain as many checkers as there are players on a team. When the signal is given, the first player on each team removes the top checker from the tower and races to the other end of the room where he lays it as a foundation for a tower on that side. He then races back, and the next in line takes a checker from the stack and puts it on the first player's checker.

Teammates race until their tower has been safely transferred from one side of the room to the other. If one player knocks down a tower, he must stop and rebuild it.

302. DROWSY WAITER

A blindfolded player, acting as the waiter, is seated on a chair in the center of the room. He holds a napkin loosely in his hands. The other players are diners and try to sneak up to snatch the napkin without being heard by the waiter.

One at a time, the diners approach as quietly as possible. If a diner is successful in grabbing the napkin before he has been heard, he becomes the waiter. However, if the waiter hears a sound, he calls out, "Stop." He then points in the direction he thinks the diner is standing. If he is correct, the diner loses his turn.

303. ROBINS AND HAWKS

One player is chosen to begin the game as a robin. All of the other players are hawks. The robin starts out from one end of the room, with a large button balanced on the tip of his little finger. This button represents the food he is trying to take to his nest. As he walks from one end of the room to his nest at the other end, the hawks flock around him, trying to cause him to lose his balance and the food. They shout at him and pretend to claw at his hand.

However, they are not permitted to touch him or the button in any way. Each player is given a turn at being the robin, and those succeeding in crossing the room without losing their food are the winners.

304. CATCH IT

This simple game can be played by a number of people, but only two can play it at one time. One person sits on top of a ladder and drops a thin sheet of paper. The other player stands on the floor and tries to catch the paper before it hits the ground. He may use only one finger and his thumb to catch the paper as it falls.

305. SIMPLE SIMON

Simple Simon is an old favorite of the children. The game leader faces the players and gives commands to them. The children are to do everything the leader tells them, if he first says, "Simon says." If the leader just says, "Touch your nose," without preceding it with, "Simon says," they must not make a move. Any child who follows an order incorrectly is out of the game.

306. Let's Take a Walk

Guests are seated in a circle with someone who is "it" in the center. "It" goes to one of the players in the circle, takes his hand and says, "Let's go for a walk." They walk around the circle for awhile, and then "it's" partner reaches for someone's hand, drawing him into the circle, and saying, "Let's go for a walk."

This continues for as long as "it" decides. However, at any time, he may call out, "Let's all go home." This is the cue for everyone to scurry for a chair. The player who is left without a place to sit becomes the new "it."

307. Sipping Race

Young children, it seems, are nearly always thirsty—especially after they have been playing actively. Take a break in the game schedule to conduct a sipping contest. Give each guest a sipping straw and a glass half-filled with some kind of soft drink. At the signal to start, each contestant begins sipping. The first one to finish is the winner.

308. Musical Chairs

Children especially love this game in its many forms, and it is a good one to play with adults as well.

Arrange chairs in a line, some facing one direction, others facing the other direction. Be sure there is at least one less chair than players.

Someone begins playing music and the contestants march around the chairs until the music stops. Each child must then scurry for a vacant chair. Any player left without a place leaves the game, and another chair is removed.

309. POISON BAG

Arrange guests in a circle and start a bean bag around. It is handed from player to player as music is being played. When the music stops, the player holding the bean bag is eliminated from the game. Continue play until only one contestant remains. In fairness, don't let the person controlling the music see the playing area.

310. MUSICAL RUGS

This is a new adaptation of the musical chairs game. Players form a circle around the game leader, standing close enough to one another to be able to pass a towel, or small rug. Distribute one towel or rug to every three players.

When the leader calls out, "All pass," players begin moving the towels about the circle until the leader calls, "All down." Players sit on their towels if they are holding one.

The last player to sit on his towel is out of the game along with any player not possessing one when the signal is given.

311. FRUIT SNATCH

This is another interesting version of musical chairs. Place a large number of oranges in a given area. Again, be sure there is one less orange than players.

As the music starts, players move in a circle around the fruit. As soon as the music stops, everyone darts into the circle to grab an orange. The player left without one leaves the game and play continues with one less orange in the pile.

312. Huckle, Buckle, Beanstalk

Send all the children from the room except for one who remains behind and hides a thimble or similar small object. When it has been hidden, the other players return to search for it. As soon as one player spots it, he sits down quietly, without telling where it is and says, "Huckle, Buckle, Beanstalk."

The one who hid the object comes over to his chair and the location is whispered. If the player is correct, he may remain seated. The game continues until everyone has located the object. Then the player who found it first is allowed to hide it, while everyone else again leaves the room.

313. Button Toss Game

This game can be played on the table or the floor and is fun for children of all ages. Use three clean, empty tin cans, a large one, a medium-sized one and a small one. Remove the lids and labels. Cut round holes in a piece of heavy cardboard so that each can is set upright in the hole. The holes should be a few inches apart and the cans placed with the bottom side up. Use a dark crayon to number the cans.

Then have players toss buttons at the cans, attempting to keep the buttons on top. Each contestant is given six tosses, with one point scored for each button remaining on the large can, two for the medium can, and three for the small one.

314. What Happened?

One player leaves the room and those remaining behind

decide on a simple event that is supposed to have happened. Help them understand that it must be something that could actually happen, and likely has. Give them some examples such as being locked out of the house, being caught in the rain, losing a mitten, finding a kitten, etc.

"It" comes back to the room and asks each player in turn, "What would you do?" The players must give an appropriate answer related to what they would do under the circumstances of the event. Each must give a different answer, as "it" attempts to discover the nature of the event.

315. FISHING AFTER SUNDOWN

Seat players on chairs that have been scattered throughout an area designated as the pond. One player is selected to be the fisherman and is blindfolded.

Give him a rope with a padded cloth sack on the end.

The fish rotate places so the fisherman will not know where each is seated. The fisherman casts out his line and the one on whom the "hook" lands must grab hold of it to be drawn toward the fisherman. The fisherman does not touch the fish but asks him three questions. "Are you a fish?" "What kind of fish?" "Are you big enough to eat?"

The fish tries to camouflage his voice, while the fisherman tries to guess which player he has on the end of his hook. If he can guess correctly, they change places. But if he is unsuccessful after three tries, he must throw the fish back into the pond. The player returns to his chair, while the fisherman makes another cast.

316. TOY SHOP

Collect about a dozen toys on a table and tell the children this will be the toy shop. Ask a volunteer to leave the room. While he is out, someone hides one of the toys. When the child is brought back and again shown the toys, he must try to tell which one is now missing.

If he can guess correctly, someone else is sent out and he gets to choose a new toy to be hidden. If he does not guess, he leaves the room to try again.

317. CUT DOWN THE ICICLES

Hang sticks of candy by strings from a heavy cord tied across one corner of the room. Each contestant is given a pair of blunt scissors, blindfolded, and instructed to cut down one piece of candy. He does this by moving forward until he thinks he is in the right place. Each player is allowed three tries.

318. MASK CREATIONS

This is an appropriate game for a Halloween party. Give each contestant a paper plate, some string, and a crayon. Each guest is told to create a mask. Help the younger children cut out holes for the eyes, nose, and mouth. When the masks are finished, each guest puts his on for a parade around the room.

319. WHO HAS THE BUTTON?

Guests are seated in a circle with someone chosen to be

"it" in the center. Give the players in the circle a button. As "it" closes his eyes, the button is passed from player to player around the circle.

"It" opens his eyes, and as the passing continues, he tries to determine who has the button. All players in the circle make this more difficult by appearing to be passing the button, whether or not they actually have it. As soon as "it" has guessed who holds the button, those two change places.

320. Beast, Bird or Fish

Seat children in a large circle with someone appointed to be "it" situated in the middle. "It" holds a bean-bag or ball, which he tosses to one of the players calling either beast, bird, or fish. As soon as the bean-bag is caught, "it" begins counting rapidly to five.

The player who caught the object must name an appropriate animal in the species named before "it" reaches five. If he does not, he must be "it." Also, if he names the wrong animal, such as a robin when fish was called, he must go to the center of the group.

321. The Dog's Bone

Players stand in a circle with one player chosen to be the dog. The dog crouches in the center of the circle with his head hidden in his arms. A toy bone or similar object is placed on the floor behind him.

The game leader points to a child in the circle, who tiptoes up to the dog to steal his bone. He then returns to his place with the bone behind him. All other players do the same in an attempt to confuse the dog. When the leader informs the dog his bone has been taken, he looks around the circle, trying to guess which player has taken it.

The dog has three tries. If he guesses correctly, the two change places.

322. What Do I See?

The children are seated in a circle. The game leader announces, "I see something red, blue, black, green, etc. What do I see?" Each player in the circle is allowed one guess at the name of the object in the room. The child who guesses correctly has a turn at choosing something for the others to guess.

323. May Basket

This is an appropriate game for little girls to play at May Day celebrations, but it is equally good for other occasions as well.

Guests are divided into two or more teams with the same number on each. Give each team a basket.

When the signal is given to begin, the first member of each team takes one flower from his basket and hands it to the next member of his team. While the first member is reaching for another flower, the second team member passes his flower along down the line to the third player and turns to get a second flower from the first player.

This continues until each flower has been taken, one at a time, from the basket and passed down to be held in the

hand of the last member on the team. When all of the
flowers are down at the end, the team begins passing—one
at a time—the flowers back along the line they came down
to the first person on the team, who then places them one
by one in the basket. The first team to get all the flowers
back in the basket is the winner.

324. GUARD THE TREASURER

Choose six players to be bodyguards. They form a circle
around the player chosen to be the treasurer. All other
players try to tag the treasurer, while the bodyguards try
to keep them away. A bodyguard is not allowed to hold or
tug a player but can only dodge at him. The first to tag the
treasurer becomes the new treasurer.

325. THE GOBLINS WILL GET YOU

This is an interesting and exciting game to be played at
a Halloween party. Select someone to be the story teller
and give him a list of names associated with Halloween.
Examples might be pumpkin, cornfield, Farmer Green,
black cat, etc. Whisper one of these names quietly to each
guest. Be sure to provide only enough chairs for the audience.

The storyteller begins the game by telling a Halloween
story, using words from the list he has been given. As each
player hears the name of the object that was whispered to
him, he must leave his chair and begin marching around
the playing area. At any time the storyteller may call out,
"The goblins will get you." When he says this, everyone

rushes for a chair. The storyteller tries to grab a chair, and the player left without a place to sit must take over as the storyteller.

This game can also be adapted for other holiday seasons by using related words in the story.

326. Look For the Bells

Before the party, hide an equal number of red and green paper cutout Christmas bells around the party area. Divide teams into the reds and the greens and send them out to search for bells the same color as their team name. After a five minute time limit, call all the players back and count the number of red bells and green ones. Be sure to warn the players that if a member of a red team brings back a green bell, it will be counted for the green team side.

327. Hidden Tree Decorations

Hide a large number of unbreakable Christmas tree decorations in fairly obvious places around the playing area. Give each child a sack and send the group out to search for ornaments. Award a candy cane to the child bringing back the most decorations. At the conclusion of the game, let each child hang the ornaments he has collected on a Christmas tree.

328. Hidden Christmas Presents

Children will especially enjoy this one, if they are old enough to read.

Wrap a simple gift for each child expected at the party and write the guest's name clearly on each. Hide the gifts around the living room.

When it is time for the gifts to be distributed, announce a treasure hunt. Be sure to instruct the children not to take a gift with someone else's name, or tell that person where he saw it hidden, but to continue searching until he finds his own gift.

329. WILD ANIMAL SAFARI

Hide cutout pictures of wild animals around the playing area. Then organize a safari to see which guest can bring back the most pictures. An appropriate prize for the winning hunter would be a box of animal crackers.

330. TELEPHONE

Players form a circle for this old favorite. The game leader whispers a relatively complicated sentence to one player, who repeats it to the person on his right. This continues on around the circle until the last player has heard the message. He then repeats it aloud.

Usually the results are a long way from the original sentence, so the two are compared. This can be tied in with a good object lesson on how facts can be distorted when a bit of gossip is passed along about someone.

331. POTATO RACE

Mark out a starting line and a finish goal. Divide players into groups of four and give each a tablespoon.

Place four potatoes at the starting line. At the signal to
go, the players race across to the goal, carrying the potatoes on the spoon. They cannot use their hands to place
the potato on the spoon, but must scoop it up. If a potato
is dropped, it may be picked up again at the spot where it
fell. This can be used as an elimination race.

332. GHOST

This is a quiet game to be played indoors. It is also an
appropriate game for traveling. The object is for one person
to begin spelling a word, using one letter. The next person
adds a second letter (one that would logically follow to
make some word), and this continues until one word has
been completed and the next person cannot think of any
letter to add to make a different one.

Specify that words must have three or more letters, and
a letter may not be added that would not be used to form
a word. When any player has collected all the letters, he is
out of the game.

333. STREETS AND ALLEYS

All players except two form parallel lines. Four or more
players should be used for each line, keeping lines just far
enough apart so the players can clasp hands in either direction. Assign two players to act as the policeman and the
robber.

As the game begins, players join hands to form streets.
The robber runs down one street, chased by the policeman.
Any time the policeman gets too close, the robber may cry,

"Alley." When he does, the players must all switch and turn in the opposite direction, joining hands with the players of a different line. This will block off the policeman, who has to run all the way around to get to the alley where the robber has gone.

Neither runner may break through the joined hands of the other players. When the policeman catches the robber, two new runners are chosen from the group.

334. JELLYBEAN TRADE

Give each player a small sack containing a dozen multi-colored jelly beans. Each player tries to get as many jelly beans of one color as he can by exchanging with the others. He decides which color he wants and then looks for some-one to trade with him.

335. FLYING BLIND

This is a game children especially enjoy. Take players one at a time and bring them to the middle of the room. Give them a chance to examine all the furniture carefully before you blindfold them and turn them around a few times so they lose their sense of direction. Then instruct the blindfolded player to locate some large object in the room, such as the front door or a chair.

336. RING TOSS

A simple ring toss game can be set up by turning chairs

upside down so that their legs protrude toward the contestants. Each leg can be given a different point value.

337. TOUCHED YOU LAST

Guests are divided into two teams and placed on two
goals. Have each team count off.

A member from one team comes out to the center area
to meet a member of the opposite team. Each carries a
newspaper rolled up to form a club. When they reach the
center, one attempts to swat the other lightly without being tagged back. If he is able to do this, he earns a point
for his team. However, should he be tagged, neither team
scores. If both are tagged in the center, they return to their
teams with no points earned.

338. HANDS FREE

Players form a circle and the leader provides articles of
varying sizes and shapes, one article for each five or six
players. Do not use anything sharp or breakable. A good
selection would be a pan, book, towel, wastebasket, etc.

When the leader blows a whistle, everyone begins
passing articles quickly around the circle. When the whistle
sounds a second time, any player holding an object or drop-
ping one must leave the circle.

If a player hesitates to accept an object offered to him,
the leader, standing in the center, may ask him to leave.
As the players drop out, take away some of the objects until finally there will be only two or three. The last player
to be counted out wins.

339. Prize Grab

Two teams line up facing each other. Have players number off—one line beginning to count from one end the other from the opposite end. This way players having the same number are standing on opposite ends.

The game leader calls out a number, and the two players with that same number race to the center, where an object has been placed. The first one there grabs the object and must race back to his line with it before he is tagged by the other.

If he is tagged, the object is returned to the center. However, if he gets back with it safely, his team scores a point before the object is returned and the game leader calls another number.

340. Soap Carving

Give each child a bar of soap and a paring knife and offer a few suggestions for carving. Information on soap carving can be obtained by writing to the Proctor and Gamble Company, Cincinnati, Ohio.

341. Flower Basket

Seat guests in a circle, with a leader in the center acting as a flower vendor. Have the guests number off by fours, calling those who are ones, roses; twos, daisies; threes, violets; and fours, tulips.

The game begins with the flower vendor calling the name of one of these four flowers. As he does, everyone belonging to that variety must change places with another from that group, with the three remaining groups keeping their places.

While the change is taking place, the vendor attempts to grab one of the places. If he is successful, the player left without a place becomes "it" for the next round.

Whenever he likes, the flower vendor may call, "Flower basket upset." When he does, everyone must scurry to find another place to sit.

342. Spin the Wheel

Seat guests in a circle of chairs. Someone is appointed to be "it," and leaves his chair to stand in the center of the circle, thus leaving his chair vacant. Contestants begin shifting down one chair at a time in an attempt to keep him from getting a new place—trying to keep a vacant chair always out of reach. When "it" succeeds in sitting in one of the chairs, the person who was supposed to move into it next is the new "it."

343. Poison Cap

Use a soft hat or similar object which can be safely passed from one person to another. One player is "it," and the game gets underway as "it" tries to tag the person holding the "poison hat."

The hat can not be thrown but must be handed from one player to another. If a person is being pursued and hands the hat to another player, that one must take it and then be chased by "it." When a player is caught, while carrying the "poison hat," he must exchange places with the person who is "it."

344. WITCH'S MAGIC WAND

Select one player to act as the witch and give her a stick for a wand. All the other players move about the playing area making unusual faces and assuming comical positions. As soon as the witch touches a player with her magic wand, that one must immediately freeze into the position he was in when touched. This continues until the witch has touched everyone in the group.

However, do not make a player remain in a frozen position longer than a few seconds.

345. CATCH THE BALLOON

Players are seated in a circle on the floor. Have them number off and place the highest number in the center to act as "it." "It" holds an inflated balloon. He suddenly drops the balloon and calls out a number.

The person with that number must try to catch the balloon before it touches the floor. If he is successful, "it" tries another number. On the other hand if a player fails to catch the balloon, he is "it."

346. WINK

Girls are seated in a circle, with a boy standing behind

each girl's chair. There should be one more boy player than there are girls, and he stands behind an empty chair.

The game proceeds with the unattached boy attempting to secure a partner by winking at the girl he wants. She responds by immediately jumping up to run to his chair. Her partner tries to prevent this by placing both hands firmly on her shoulders.

If the lone boy fails in one attempt, he winks at another player. When a girl succeeds in getting away, she leaves an empty chair and the boy behind it must wink at another girl to get a new partner.

Each boy must keep his hands behind the back of the chair at all times until it is necessary to reach for his partner, and then he is only allowed to place both hands on her shoulders. After awhile, boys and girls may change places, with the game proceeding as before.

347. Jelly Bean Target

Players choose partners. Give one of them a dozen jelly beans. One partner acts as a target, standing with his mouth wide open. He tries to catch beans that are thrown to him. The couple with the most completed tosses wins.

348. Lost

Seat guests in a circle of chairs and appoint someone as "it" to wait in the center. Place a selection of familiar objects in the center of the circle, such as a spoon, book, ball, fan, or anything with a blunt edge. Provide enough objects for all but two or three of the contestants.

"It" begins passing the objects around the circle in the
same direction. He has a list of the available objects, and
once they have begun rotating around the circle, he may
call out any two objects from the list.

The two players holding those objects called must immediately jump up and attempt to change places with one
another. While this is happening, "it" tries to steal one of
their chairs. If he is successful, the one without a place to
sit becomes "it."

349. OUR HOUSE IS TUMBLING DOWN

Divide players into two equal groups. Each group gets
together to select some part of a house or furnishings, which
is to be symbolized by the first letter of its name. The two
teams then line up at opposite ends of the room and advance until they are four or five feet from each other.

If Team One had selected the word "Chimney," the captain of the team would call, "Our house is tumbling down
for want of a C." The other team then names words associated with a house, beginning with the letter C, such as
closet, cupboard, chair, carpet.

When chimney is named, players from Team One race
back to their end of the room with players of Team Two
attempting to tag them. All who are caught must join Team
Two for the next round.

352. SPIN THE PLATTER

Players are seated in a circle and numbered. One person

chosen to be "it" stands in the center holding a pie tin or similar object.

As the game begins, "it" gives the tin a good spin and calls out a number. The player with that number must run to the center of the circle and catch the platter before it falls over. If he succeeds, he may return to his seat. Otherwise, he becomes "it."

Be sure the chairs are just far enough from the center to make it difficult for players to get quickly to the platter. Also, "it" may spin the platter at any place in the circle he wishes, thus he may be quite far from the number he intends to call.

PART SIX

•
•
•

DON'T FORGET THE SUNTAN LOTION

The beach and swimming area offer such a wide variety of recreational possibilities, one might believe a planned game schedule unnecessary. However, when a beach party is on the agenda at summer camp, or just to provide an extra measure of fun for the swimsuit set, games especially programmed for use on the waterfront will be greatly enjoyed.

When staging swimming relays, be sure to warn contestants about water safety, as it might be quite easy for them to become so enthusiastic that they ignore usual precautions.

Plan adequate rest periods between strenuous activities.

And for those long, pleasant hours in the sun, don't forget the suntan lotion!

353. Mole Search

Mark off a boundary area in the sand, not too large, in which blindfolded players conduct a search on hands and knees. Toss a shoe or similar harmless object into the enclosure and instruct each "mole" to find it. A good idea would be to station monitors around the boundary lines to guide the strays back into the circle.

354. Water Boy

Each contestant holds a container filled with water and lines up on a designated starting point. The objective of the relay is to have the contestants hop, keeping both feet locked tightly together at all times, to the opposite goal line. The winner is not necessarily the one who gets to the goal first, but the one who gets there first with the most water in his container .

355. Canoe Combat

This contest must be carefully supervised, and it should be greatly enjoyed by spectators as well as by those in the competition. Contestants work in pairs, with two in a canoe, and only two canoes involved at one time.

While one contestant paddles, the other holds a long pole. The end of the pole must be carefully wrapped in several thicknesses of burlap so it is well padded. This is the only part of the pole that may be used.

The contest is to see which team can push the other out of its canoe.

356. DIGGING FOR TREASURE

If you have access to a secluded sandy beach, secretly bury a box of treasure containing trinkets, chewing gum, pennies, etc. Then instruct players to go down to the beach and dig for buried treasure. Point out the area in which the treasure has been hidden a few inches below the sand.

A good idea would be to rake over the area, outlining where digging should be done. This would serve to completely cover any marks made by the burying. You could provide cleverly designed treasure maps outlining the correct digging area.

357. INNER TUBE RELAY

Divide players into two or more teams and give each team an inflated inner tube. At the signal to begin, the first contestant on each team picks up the tube, pulls it down over his head past his body, and then steps out of it. As quickly as he can do this, he moves out of the way for the second contestant on his team to repeat the procedure. This continues down the line until a winning team is determined.

358. WATERFRONT FOOTBALL

Using ropes and floats to mark off the boundary lines, stage a football game in water about waist deep. A rubber football should be used.

Do not allow for repeated first downs, but when a team has possession of the ball, it is allowed only four downs. If

the team fails to score in four downs, they must either kick
or give up the ball on downs to the other side. As the ball
is played in water, you may permit tackling, blocking, and
all the usual action on the football field.

359. BEACH BALL KEEP-AWAY

Organize a keep-away game with the twist that each time
a whistle is blown, team players may only use one hand and
arm in their keep-away attempts until the all clear whistle
is sounded again a short time later.

Any contestant using both hands or arms during the
handicapped period is eliminated from competition.

360. CORK RETRIEVE

Toss out several dozen corks into deep water. When a
whistle is blown, have your good swimmers go out after
them. Scatter the corks over a wide enough area to make
the game interesting.

First prize is awarded to the swimmer retrieving the
most corks. For added zest, corks could be dabbed with
colored paint, with the different colors designating earning
points, and the score tallied in this way.

361. TURTLE RACE

If there are small turtles available in the area, give your
guests time to capture a few. Each contestant who finds one

within the time limit is allowed to enter his racer in prize competition.

Mark off a large circle in the sand for the racing area. Place turtles under a large bucket, until the signal is given to start. When the signal is given, the bucket is lifted. Turtles may not be touched in any way.

The first turtle to cross the outer edge of the circle is declared the winner.

362. WATER BRONCO

Toss an empty, tightly capped, fifty gallon drum into water deep enough for it to float. Then stage a water rodeo by determining which rider can remain astride the drum for the longest time period. This will require considerable skill, as the drum will tip over easily unless carefully balanced. Be sure to use a stop watch to clock each contestant.

363. BALLOON SCOOT

Line up racers at a goal and give each an inflated balloon or light rubber ball. This must be pushed in front of him across the water, using only his nose as he races across a specified area.

364. SPOON AND BALL RACE

Players must be able to do the backstroke for this interesting race. Equip each swimmer with a tablespoon and a rubber ball.

When the signal is given, each swimmer puts the handle
of the spoon in his mouth, places the ball on the bowl of
the spoon, and then swims toward the goal. If the ball falls
off the spoon, the swimmer must stop to replace it before
continuing competition.

365. CANDLE SWIM

Give each contestant a lighted candle, which he is to hold
out of the water with one hand while swimming from a
starting line to the goal. If a swimmer's candle is extinguished at any point along the way, he is disqualified.

366. ARTILLERY

If there is a large beach ball available, this is an interesting waterfront game to include in the recreation schedule. Divide the contestants into two teams and stand each
team on an opposite firing line with about fifty feet between the two. Team members stand close together in a
straight line. The first member of one team is given a beach
ball with instructions to "fire" at the opposite team. He
must throw the ball high into the air so that the ball will
come down on the opposing team.

Members being bombarded may not move out of position. Anyone struck by the ball must go to join the other
team. As soon as one team has fired, the other team has a
try. Or, you might permit a team to fire again after each
successful hit.

367. Greased Watermelon Contest

Coat a large watermelon with grease and float it out onto the water. Divide the group into two equal sides, establish goals, and instruct each side to try to get the watermelon to its goal. Or, you could award the watermelon to the team having it in possession as it is brought onto the beach.

368. Fishing Fun

Mark out a restricted area in water not over waist deep, placing someone as fisherman in the center. When the fisherman gives a predetermined signal, all the "fish" move out into the playing area.

If any fish is tagged, he must join the fisherman in trying to catch the others as they come across the playing area next time. The goals on either end are safety zones for the fish. Fish may either walk past the fisherman or dive underwater until they have passed the fishing zone.

If you are careful to keep the playing area small enough, this can be a most interesting water game.

369. Diving For Pearls

If the water is clear and the bottom quite smooth, stage a pearl diving contest. Scatter a large quantity of glass marbles in the water and see who is able to gather the biggest pile of them.

This will be especially enjoyed by younger children, and is a good idea for parents to use in helping their children overcome fear of the water.

370. MELON KEEP AWAY

Another version of keep away is to toss a large melon to the swimmers and have a few judges on hand to keep time in determining which side has longest possession of the melon. Award the melon as a prize to that side.

371. ONE MAN IN A TUB

Set up a contest to determine who can remain afloat in a large wash tub for the longest time. This requires balancing, so competition will most likely narrow down to two or three contestants. This contest will be enjoyed by spectators, too.

372. SNORKLE CONTEST

Each contestant gets a large drinking straw, which he puts in his mouth to breathe through under water. When the signal is given, each contestant submerges. The straw must be held with one end of the water so a contestant can breathe through it. The swimmer staying underwater longest is declared the winner.

373. POISON DEN

Make a small circle or pit in the sand and place a beach ball in the center of it. Have players hold hands around the circle and move in a circular direction. The circle will move

in and out toward the "poison den," as each player tries to
force one of the others into it. When anyone is forced inside,
the other players immediately drop their hands and dash
for a safety zone.

The one who is in the den grabs the beach ball and tries
to hit one of the fleeing players before he gets back to
safety. When he succeeds, the one who is hit is out of the
game. But if the thrower fails to hit another player, he is
out of the game.

374. Bulls-eye Dive

Float a large inner tube in the water under the diving
board. Each diver has three tries to get from the board
through the tube. Be sure to keep the valve inside the tube.
Otherwise, you can tape the valve to the side of the inner
tube to keep it out of the way.

375. Lights Out

Two contestants meet in a playing area; each one carrying a lighted candle. The object of the game is to attempt
to blow out the other contestant's candle while keeping
his own burning. This can be worked nicely into a tournament if the group is not too large. If both candles are blown
out at the same time, give the contestants another try.

376. Rooster Warfare

Mark out a circle in the sand about five or six feet in

diameter and place two contestants in the center. These are the roosters who must squat on their heels and keep both arms folded. The object of the contest is to see which "bird" can shove the other out of the circle. If desired this can be set up on the basis of the best two out of three attempts to stay inside.

PART SEVEN

●
●
●

DOES ANYONE HAVE A PENCIL?

Written games can have an important place in the successful party program. For adult players, they may bring back nostalgic classroom memories. For everyone taking part, they are a challenge to both memory and wit.

Most of the paper and pencil games included in this chapter are described as team projects. When players participate in a team effort, the pressure is taken from individual achievement. Start a number of players thinking together, and the old adage, "two heads are better than one" is proven true. However, if the group is quite small, any of the written games described can be adapted for players working alone.

377. Concentrated Vocabulary

Players are divided into teams with a team captain appointed for each. Captains have a pencil and pad of paper. Allow teams five minutes in which to list all the words they can which sound like one letter of the alphabet. The word should be listed properly along with the alphabet letter. These can be proper names, such as K for Kay, D for Dee, J for Jay. Some other examples could be U for you, T for tea, C for sea.

378. Which Came First?

With some careful study before the party, you can develop an interesting game using the chronology of characters and events related in the Bible. Give each guest a paper and pencil and then list a number of people or happening from the Bible. Guests must rearrange them in proper order.

379. Look Into the Future

Contestants are divided into two teams and seated in rows facing each other. Give guests a slip of paper and pencil with instructions to write a twenty-five word prophecy of what is going to happen to the person in the opposite row. When everyone has finished, collect the slips and redistribute them. They must be folded and not read until the proper time.

Have the first member of one line ask the person oppo-

site him, "What will my future be?" That person then
reads the information written on the slip of paper he holds.
When he has finished, he asks the same question. The person opposite him then reads the prophecy he has been
given. This continues down the rows until each person has
been questioned and had a chance to read his slip of paper.

380. BIBLE OCCUPATIONS

Supply each guest with a piece of paper and pencil.
Within a specified time limit see how many Bible characters each can list along with the correct occupation of each
character.

381. BABY ANIMALS

This would be an appropriate written game to play at a
baby shower. The group is divided into small teams and
given a pad and pencil. One member of the team numbers
the paper from one to fifteen. The game leader then calls
out the name of an animal.

Teams must try to name the proper term to the young
of that species. If you prefer to do this on an individual
basis, have the list printed and allow a five minute period
for guests to fill in the name of the baby animals. Here is a
suggested list:

1. sheep   1. lamb
2. goose   2. gosling
3. lion   3. cub
4. bear   4. cub

5. swan	5. cygnet
6. whale	6. calf
7. cat	7. kitten
8. horse	8. foal
9. frog	9. polliwog, tadpole
10. seal	10. calf
11 dog	11. puppy
12. deer	12. fawn
13. kangaroo	13. joey
14. duck	14. duckling
15. bull seal	15. bachelor

382. Animal Mates

Conduct this game in the same manner as the one listed previously, using names of male and female in a species. The game leader calls out the name of an animal, allowing time for the teams to list the proper names of the male and female of each. A list is given below:

Male	Female
1. tiger	1. tigress
2. ram	2. ewe
3. stallion	3. mare
4. fox	4. vixen
5. stag	5. hind
6. buck	6. doe
7. peacock	7. peahen
8. bull	8. cow
9. gander	9. goose
10. drake	10. duck
11. jackass	11. jenny
12. boar	12. sow

383. Famous Couples

Here is another good game for bridal showers or wedding aniversary celebrations. Each guest is given a paper and pencil and asked to see how many famous couples he is able to list from the Bible, from history, and from the modern world.

384. Is This From the Bible?

Select a number of well-known quotations similar in tone to those found in Scripture. List these with some actually found in the books of Ecclesiastes and Proverbs. Mix the two and read them to your guests to see how many can be correctly identified.

385. List the Errors

Read a familiar Bible story with several errors in names and places written in. As the story is read, guests are to write down any mistakes they catch.

386. Name the Book

Prepare a selection of Bible incidents which appear in only one book of the Old or New Testament. Divide guests into teams and see which team can correctly identify the most incidents with their proper book in the Bible.

387. Bible Names and Bible Places

Each guest prints his first and last name down one edge of a sheet of paper. Within a specified time, contestants are to list as many proper names of people or places found in the Bible that he can think of beginning with the letters in his name.

388. Waiting for the Baby

This would be an interesting game to use at a baby shower and will most likely stump many of the players. Using the list given below, prepare a similar sheet for each guest with names of animals on the left and their incubation period proceeded by alphabetical letters on the right. Mix them around and have the contestants attempt to match them properly.

Animals	Incubation Period
1. cow	A. 9½ months
2. elephant	B. 21 months
3. sheep	C. 3 months
4. horse	D. 11 months
5. rabbit	E. 1 month
6. cat	F. 2 months
7. goose	G. 26 days
8. goat	H. 150 days
9. hen	I. 21 days
10. giraffe	J. 14 months
11. opossum	K. 13 days
12. human	L. 280 days

389. Books of the Bible

Test your guests by having them see how many books of the Bible each can list in a given length of time. You might limit this to either the Old Testament or the New Testament.

390. Right or Wrong Spelling

Select several difficult proper names from the Bible and list them on sheets of paper. Misspell some of them. Then give each contestant paper and pencil before you spell aloud the names you have listed. Using a consecutive number for each word, guests indicate whether you have spelled the word correctly or incorrectly.

391. Cost of Living

This is a game to play at a party honoring a newly married couple or for a wedding anniversary celebration. Using an ad from a local store, list some staple foods such as butter, eggs, potatoes, milk, bread, etc. Then on the opposite side, in different order, list the prices charged for these items. See how many guests can correctly match the price with the article.

392. Go Togethers

Give each guest a paper and pencil to use in listing as

many affinities as possible. Some possibilities are:
1. Salt and pepper
2. Paint and brush
3. Husband and wife
4. Needle and thread
5. Pen and ink
6. Table and chair
7. Bread and butter

393. MISINFORMED EXPERTS

Guests will need paper and pencil for this one, too. Assign one subject to the men and another to the women. Within a specified time, everyone is to write all he knows about the subject. Be sure to give the men a subject such as how to bake a prizewinning cake and the women something like the operation of a combustible engine.

394. REWRITE THE NURSERY RHYME

List several different nursery rhymes on separate pieces of paper. The last line of each should be omitted. Pass the rhymes around to your guests with instructions that each is to come up with his own version of the last line. These should be as comical as possible. When everyone is finished, collect the papers and read them aloud.

395. GIVING THANKS

Each guest prints the words "My Reasons For Thanksgiving" across the top of a sheet of paper. Within a time limit, each guest lists as many things as possible to be thankful for—using only the letters which appear in that statement. A letter may not be used more times than it appears in the statement, so instruct them to cross it off as a letter is used.

396. CHRISTMAS PRESENTS

Instruct each contestant to print his name down the edge of a sheet of paper. Using the letters of his name to begin each word, he jots down a list of Christmas presents. A person named Lester Roberts might include:

L unch pail
E ar muff
S oldering gun
T elescope
E lephant
R ake
R ailroad
O rgan
B aseball
E gg beater
R ing
T op
S top watch

397. HOLIDAY TELEGRAMS

Have each guest print MERRY CHRISTMAS, HAPPY NEW YEAR, HAPPY HALLOWEEN, whichever greeting is appropriate to the holiday being celebrated. Then instruct everyone to write a telegram beginning with each of the letters in the greeting.

398. YEAR'S END NEWS ROUNDUP

At a New Year's Eve party, pass around a pencil and paper to each contestant. See who can list the most major news events occurring during the past year. News could be limited to local events only, or perhaps important events which occurred within your church.

399. CHRISTMAS VOCABULARY

At your Christmas party, see how many four letter words can be listed from the greeting MERRY CHRISTMAS. No letter may be used any more often than it appears in these two words. This is also a good idea to use at other seasonal parties, or with the names of honored guests.

400. THESE FACTS MAKE CENTS

Give each guest a Lincoln head penny, pencil, and a piece of paper, along with the following list. Allow a set time limit to see how many can find the information listed.

1. The name of a country. (America)
2. An oriental fruit. (Date)
3. A large body of water. (C—sea)
4. A rabbit. (Hare—hair)

5. The top of a hill. (Brow)
6. A messenger. (One cent—one sent)
7. A beverage. (T—tea)
8. Flowers. (Tulips—two lips)
9. Part of a bird. (Feathers)
10. A part of corn. (Ear)
11. A sacred place. (Temple)
12. A statement of faith. (In God we trust.)
13. Portion of a river. (Mouth)
14. The ego. (I—eye)
15. An application of paint. (Coat)

401 EDUCATED TOUCH

Guests are blindfolded and seated in a circle. Pass a
dozen familiar objects, one after another, around the group.
As soon as each guest has held all the objects, take them
from the room and remove the blindfolds. Then see how
many objects each guest can list on a piece of paper within
a five minute time limit.

402. WITTY EXHIBIT

Arrange several of the objects listed below in an exhibit.
Allow guests several moments to look over the objects before you take them away. Give each contestant a piece of
paper on which you have listed a number of descriptions.
Each guest writes the name of the item he has just examined, which best fits each description listed.

Here are a few you might use.

1. Box of dates. (Calendar in a box)

2. Big cut ups. (Two large scissors)
3. Book of numbers. (Telephone directory)
4. A drive through the wood. (Nail partially driven in piece of wood)
5. Tax on tea. (Tacks placed on a package of tea)
6. Missionary. (Penny—"One sent")
7. A swimming match. (Match floating on water)
8. Counterpoints. (Two straight pins crossed at their points)
9. An endless subject. (A ring)
10. The four seasons. (Four cans of seasoning)
11. Something to adore. (A key to a door)
12. Redskins. (Two ripe tomatoes)
13. The awful truth. (A mirror)
14. The birthplace of Burns. (An electric iron)
15. Musical group. (A rubber band)

403. Occupation Stones

Give your guests a list of occupations with instructions to write the name of a well known stone which fits each one.

1. Undertaker (Tombstone)
2. Coward (Yellowstone)
3. Surgeon (Bloodstone)
4. Dairyman (Milkstone)
5. German Fisherman (Rhinestone)
6. Architect (Cornerstone)
7. Motorist (Milestone)
8. Demanding boss (Grindstone)
9. Standard bearer (Flagstone)
10. Coolie (Lodestone)

11. Locksmith (Keystone)
12. Shoemaker (Cobblestone)
13. Politician (Blarney stone)
14. Laundryman (Soapstone)
15. Citrus grower (Limestone)

404. ROMAN NUMERALS

List a number of Roman numerals in high figures and see how many guests can accurately decipher them into Arabic numerals.

405. MEMORY TEST

Show the players a tray containing a number of well-known objects. A set of keys, a pen, a powder compact, one earring, a button, a class ring, a watch, a piece of string, etc. Let the guests examine the objects carefully for one minute. Then take the assortment away and allow each player five minutes to list on a piece of paper as many of the things he can remember.

406. QUICK THINKING

When the signal to begin has been given, each guest writes down the first ten objects that come to his mind. The first to complete his list is the winner, but allow the other players to finish. Then go around the circle and have each player read the ten objects he put down. The results should be quite interesting.

407. ADVERTISING SLOGANS

Gather about a dozen familiar advertising slogans from a magazine or newspaper and write them down. Read the list to your guests, assigning the slogans a number to see how many each person can identify correctly.

408. SUPPLY THE MISSING WORD

On slips of paper, write out the statements given in the list below, leaving off the last word. Each guest tries to see how many of the missing words he can add correctly.

1. Skinny as a _____ (rail)
2. Quiet as a _____ (mouse)
3. Hard as a _____ (rock)
4. Pretty as a _____ (picture)
5. Neat as a _____ (pin)
6. Smart as a _____ (whip)
7. Fat as a _____ (pig)
8. Hungry as a _____ (bear)
9. Innocent as a _____ (baby)
10. Spry as a _____ (kitten)

409. ORIGINAL COLONIES

See how many of the original thirteen colonies in America each guest can list. Be sure to include New York, Pennsylvania, Deleware, New Jersey, North Carolina, South Carolina, Maryland, Virginia, Georgia, Rhode Island, New Hampshire, Massachusetts and Connecticut.

410. RECOGNIZE THE STATES

Trace out the states from a large map. Do not identify them in any way other than by their outline. Then put them up on display, giving each a number and see how many each guest is able to correctly identify.

411. COLOR AND OBJECT

Collect a number of differently colored objects that can be easily identified. Hold them up one at a time and give everyone a chance to see them. Then remove the objects and pass out paper and pencil to see how many of the objects—as well as the correct color of each—players can list. To earn one point, the objects and its correct color must be listed.

412. GUESS HOW FAR

Sometime before the party, measure in inches the distance between certain points in the living room. Keep this information written down and when it is time for this game, ask the guests to attempt to estimate the distance between the various objects. A possible idea would be to have players total the inches in their guesses, and the one who comes closest to the correct total would be the winner.

413. WHAT WAS HE WEARING?

Dress one guest in elaborate attire and bring him into

the room so that all the contestants are allowed a good,
long look. When he leaves, pass out papers and pencils and
tell your guests to list as many articles of clothing with
color description, etc., that they can recall seeing.

414. Mother Goose Says

Write only the first line of a Mother Goose rhyme on
slips of paper and pass around several to each player. See
who is able to complete the most rhymes in a designated
period of time.

415. Speed Writing

Use a stop watch for this one, or the minute hand on
a clock. When the signal is given to begin, each contestant
begins writing the numbers from one as far as he can get
before one minute has elapsed.

416. Tree Species

See how many different species of trees each guest can
list within a specified time. One could also use flowers,
fruits, animals, and birds.

417. Ten Kates

Read the following ten questions to your guests. Explain

that the answer to each has the sound of Kate in it.
1. What Kate is always repeating herself? (duplicate)
2. What Kate makes wheels go round? (lubricate)
3. What Kate is always making speeches at ceremonies for the opening of new buildings? (dedicate)
4. What Kate chews her food well? (masticate)
5. What Kate is always out of breath? (suffocate)
6. What Kate is full of advice? (advocate)
7. What Kate is good at finding things? (locate)
8. What Kate is able to get out of difficult situations? (extricate)

418. It's a Man's World

Here is a similar list using the word man. However, these are tricky.
1. A man with an appointment. (mandate)
2. A literary man. (manuscript)
3. A Chinese man. (mandarin)
4. A traveling man. (mango)
5. A married man. (Herman)
6. A small man. (manikin)
7. A musical man. (mandolin)
8. A stable man. (man'ger)
9. A mixed up man. (mangle)

419. Famous Sayings

Each contestant has a pencil and paper to list which famous person originated the well-known saying you will read aloud. Or you may have them printed for each contestant, if you want to allow a bit more time to work on the answers.

1. "Give me liberty or give me death." (Patrick Henry)
2. "Ask not what your country can do for you, but rather what you can do for your country." (John F. Kennedy)
3. "A penny saved is a penny earned." (Benjamin Franklin)
4. "I can promise you only blood, sweat and tears." (Winston Churchill)
5. "A thing of beauty is a joy forever." (Keats)
6. "I came, I saw, I conquered." (Julius Caesar)
7. "Old soldiers never die, they just fade away." (Douglas MacArthur)
8. "To die is gain." (Paul)
9. "A rose by any other name would smell as sweet." (William Shakespeare)
10. "My only regret is that I have but one life to give to my country." (Nathan Hale)
11. "If the people can't eat bread, let them eat cake." (Marie Antoinette)
12. "We are not amused." (Queen Victoria)
13. "All I know is just what I read in the papers." (Will Rogers)
14. "I would rather be right than president." (Henry Clay)
15. "I have not yet begun to fight." (John Paul Jones)

420. STATE-MENTS

Pass out slips of paper on which are written the following statements and see how many can list the proper state after each. The answer may be either the full name of a state or its official abbreviation.

1. The state that has been behind bars. (Conn.)
2. The state that did not pay its bills. (Iowa)
3. The state that could withstand a flood. (Ark.)
4. The state that is busiest on Monday. (Wash.)
5. The spinster state. (Miss.)
6. The state that could move a boat. (Ore.)
7. The state with good vision. (Tennessee)
8. The state that is always yourself. (Me.)
9. The state that needs a doctor. (Ill.)
10. The state that is watched by the Internal Revenue Service. (Texas)

421. Art Colony

Pass out paper and pencils to the guests and ask each to draw the head of a man, woman, or child at the top of the page. The paper is then folded so only the bottom of the neck is left showing. The papers are then passed to the person seated to the left of each guest and the shoulders are added before the paper is folded again.

As papers move from player to player, the waist, hips, legs, and feet are added. Be sure to caution the colony of artists not to look at the work that has already been done on their sketch. When the drawings are completed, unfold the papers and pass them around so everyone can have a look.

422. History Lesson

Read the list of famous events in history and literature

given below and see how many of them the guests can
identify.

1. He was marooned on a deserted island (Robinson
   Crusoe)
2. She wore a glass slipper. (Cinderella)
3. He flew a kite in a storm. (Benjamin Franklin)
4. He stood before a burning bush. (Moses)
5. He laid his cloak over a mud puddle. (Sir Walter
   Raleigh)
6. He invented the cotton gin. (Eli Whitney)
7. He was the founder of the United States Navy. (John
   Paul Jones)
8. He played his fiddle while his city burned. (Emporer
   Nero)
9. He was the first European to discover the Pacific ocean.
   (Balboa)
10. He pounded his shoe on the table at a world conference.
    (Nikita Khrushchev.)

PART EIGHT

●
●
●

PENNY FOR YOUR THOUGHTS

All but one of the dozen "mind reading" games included in this section require the assistance of an accomplice. Be sure to explain trick procedures carefully to this person sometime before the game begins so everything will run smoothly.

Much of the success in stumping your audience depends on the skill used in a subtle cover up of secret cues and prearranged presentation of the performance. If you succeed in disguising obvious hints with a glib tongue and quick hand, more than one baffled guest may offer a "penny for your thoughts."

423. Pick the Fruit

Send your accomplice from the room. While he is
gone, instruct the audience to choose some type of fruit.
When he comes back, enumerate several different kinds of
fruit. You tip off your partner by having him say "yes" to
the first kind of fruit listed after you have named some
small fruit.

If the group had chosen pineapple, just before you asked
if the fruit picked was pineapple, you ask if the one they
had chosen was strawberry. This will work even if the
group itself should pick a small fruit to be guessed, as you
would then list two small types of fruit one after the other,
with the second small fruit being correct.

424. The Mind Reader and His Cane

This mind reading game is a bit complicated to perform,
but it will be sure to stump any guests who have not seen
it done before.

One person with a cane or stick waits with the group
while the mind reader leaves the room. The two have a
plan previously worked out, which follows that the first
letter in any word stressed gives the consonants in the
word to be guessed.

The cane is tapped to spell out vowels. One tap for an
a, two for an e, three for an i, four for an o and five for
a u. If the word chosen is chair, use words beginning with
c, h and r to stress. Tap once for the a and three times for
the i. This should be accompanied with a great deal of
dialogue in an attempt to cover up what is being done, but

not too much to confuse the mind reader who eventually guesses any word chosen by the group.

425. THIS OR THAT

Send your accomplice from the room and have players select a visible object in the room. When your helper returns, point out different objects asking, "Is it this," he will answer, "No," until the correct object is pointed out and you ask, "Is it that?"

Or, to make it a bit more difficult to catch, the chosen object could be pointed out with the second "that."

426. ALEXANDER THE MIND READER

Have everyone in the group write out short questions on slips of paper, explaining that they will be read by Alexander the Greatest.

Alexander picks out a folded slip and rubs it once across his forehead, going through a great deal of pretended concentration. He then calls out a question and gives his answer to it. A person previously instructed in the crowd reacts with amazement, claiming that was his question and thanking Alexander for answering it.

Alexander nonchalantly checks the paper to be sure, and in this way is able to read a question some other guests has written on it. He discards the paper, picks up a new folded slip and gives the question he just read.

Of course, the person who had written the question is quite surprised, including the other guests who hear their questions read aloud and answered.

427. Read the Ashes

This is a clever mind trick and very simple to do. However, it might take your audience some time to catch on, if they have not seen it done before.

One person poses as a mind reader. He holds several slips of paper, and as each guest comes up to him one at a time, he has them whisper the name of a famous person in his ear. He pretends to write this name on a slip.

The paper is then folded and placed in a large tin can. What he actually has done, however, is written the name given to him by the first guest on each slip of paper. Then, while the mind reader's back is turned, someone draws a slip from the collection. All other papers are burned to ashes in a flat tin can. After they have cooled, the mind reader, with a great deal of concentrated effort, sifts through the ashes, studying them carefully. He then tells the name of the famous person written on the slip of paper that was not burned.

Of course, it is the same one written on each slip.

428. What Time Is It?

The leader sends a confederate from the room and decides with the group on an hour to be guessed. Sometime between one and twelve.

When the accomplice returns, the leader makes a statement such as "I can not tell you this time."

The accomplice then asks, "Was it three o'clock?"

Everyone will be quite amazed, as three was the right time chosen. Actually it is very simply done. The second word of the sentence the leader says should begin with the letter of the alphabet that is the same number from A as the time chosen. A is first, so it would be 1:00 o'clock, B would be 2:00, etc.

429. MAGIC COLOR

Sometime beforehand the leader and his accomplice decide on a magic color. When it is time for the stunt, the accomplice is sent from the room while the rest of the group tells the leader an article or a person they have chosen to be guessed.

When the confederate returns, the leader points to some object and person asking, "It is this?"

The accomplice is able to answer yes or no correctly every time, because the next object pointed out by the leader, after an article the color previously determined will be the right one. For example, the correct article might always follow a red object, red dress, vase, etc.

A variation on this would be to use four legged object just before the correct object.

430. WHICH GUEST HAS THE PENNY?

Place a penny on a dish. The mind reader leaves the room, while his secret assistant waits with the group. While he is away, any member of the group is chosen to pick up the penny and hold it in his hand.

When the mind reader returns, he asks guests to come one at a time and place their index finger on the plate. Each finger is studied carefully.

The mind reader has no trouble spotting the person who
has the penny, since his assistant placed his finger on the
plate the next one after the one who has the coin.

431. NAME THE CITY

Ask your partner to leave the room and have the group
select the name of a city to be identified. Arrange beforehand that you will list a number of cities but the correct
one will immediately follow one with a color in it.

If this seems a bit obvious after a few tries, switch to another clue. The next clue might be that the correct city
would follow one containing two parts such as New York,
South Bend or Santa Barbara. To further confuse the audience, have a few other clues on hand.

432. INVISIBLE INK

By using a quill pen and lemon juice you can write
secret messages on plain sheets of white paper. At first
glance, the sheets appear to be blank. However, when
they have been carefully warmed over a flame, the writing
will mysteriously appear. A number of sentences could be
written on different slips of paper and handed to each guest
to decipher and then read aloud to the group.

433. WAVE THE MAGIC WAND

Work with a confederate on this one, explaining to him
before you begin that the first letter of the first word in

each statement you make will spell out in correct order the letters of the word chosen.

When the accomplice leaves, a word is picked. As he returns, begin waving a stick or ruler in elaborate fashion as you make appropriate statements. Guests will try to connect the stick waving with guessing and are not so likely to notice the order of words used.

Be sure to leave a long enough pause between each statement so your accomplice will not become confused.

434. MINDREADING INSTRUCTIONS

Arrange with a woman guest to act as your confederate. When it comes time for this mind reading game, send her from the room as the guests choose an action for her to perform. It might be to sneeze, or sing, rub her head, or turn around.

When the mind reader returns, she sits down while you stand behind her. No words are spoken, but you begin to slowly rub your hands across her forehead.

The secret of the trick is very simple. Each time your hands are drawn back, you are spelling a letter. Draw them back one time for a, twice for b, three times for c. When a letter has been counted out, pause, perhaps pressing lightly so she will know you have come to the end of the letter.

She has merely to keep track of the letters until the word has been spelled out, and she can then correctly follow the instructions.

PART NINE

●
●
●

TRICKS BEFORE TREATS

The stunts included in this section are simple to perform and do not require elaborate props or background. Most of them utilize equipment readily available and are simple to explain.

Stunt time affords an opportunity to clown and show off a bit. A planned assortment of stunts can bring the party games to a merry conclusion. So just before you treat your guests to refreshments, throw in a few stunt tricks for fun.

435. RIDICULOUS REFLECTIONS

If possible, arrange for a large frame for this hilarious new stunt. One could quite easily be cut from one side of a large cardboard box. Ask for volunteers—a boy and a girl —and work with only one or two couples at a time.

The boy acts as his partner's mirrored reflection, as she goes through the motions of putting on makeup and combing her hair. He must attempt to exactly duplicate her actions and facial expressions.

Caution the girl to move a bit more slowly than usual to help in the imitation.

436. SHADOW SURGERY

For this stunt, you will need to suspend a large white sheet between the audience and your "working" area. This can be accomplished by tying up a length of clothesline and using clothespins to hang the sheet.

All the lights are extinguished, except for one bright light behind the sheet. This will cause sharply outlined silhouettes to fall on the sheet. Place a table behind the curtain and assemble as many odd instruments and gimmicks as you will need to make the stunt enjoyable.

As the play begins, a patient is brought into the operating table. Next, two nurses and a doctor come on the scene. As the three perform the operation, they go to great lengths in describing what they are doing. Use a book for the brain —a clock for the heart. All can be carefully examined. If the patient regains consciousness from time to time, a whack on the head will put him back "out." The possibilities are as many as they are fun.

437. WALK THE PLANK

Send guests from the room and bring them back one at a time. A board is placed between two chairs, just above a tub half-filled with water. As each guest is brought back in, he is shown the plank and the tub of water. Then he is blindfolded as two "pirates" lift him to the plank.

He is told that he must walk the plank and jump into the tub. Once the contestant has been carefully blindfolded, the tub is quietly removed and replaced with a pile of soft pillows. Assist relunctant guests with a gentle push.

438. FEED THE BABY

Guests are divided into pairs and brought to a table where they are both blindfolded. Provide each with a small bowl of pudding, a spoon, and bib. Each contestant is to attempt to feed the pudding to the other.

439. STRONG MAN

A good test of strength for the men at your party is to see how many are able to lift a chair by gripping only one of its legs. It's not as easy as it may sound.

440. THE MOST ASTONISHING THREAD

The day before your party, submerge about a foot of ordinary wrapping cord in a cup containing a well-mixed

solution that is fifty percent water and fifty percent salt.
Soak the cord for a considerable time, and then remove it
to dry thoroughly.

When the party is underway, give guests an opportunity
to examine the cord for any hidden wire. Then tie one end
of the thread to a metal object and at the other end, tie a
metal ring. Ignite the string. Your guests will be amazed as
the string, which apparently goes up in flames, continues
to support the ring.

441. MIDNIGHT SNACK

Although only two players can participate in this stunt,
it will be greatly enjoyed by the spectators as well. Blindfold two volunteers and seat them on the floor an arm's
reach from one another. Each is given two crackers which
they attempt to feed to each other . . . at the same time.

442. POLE VAULTING STUNT

A contestant holding a broomstick in both hands is instructed to jump over it. This is quite a difficult trick. The
secret of success lies in the fact that, the moment one jumps,
he must thrust both hands downward.

443. STICKY DIME STUNT

This stunt should provide a lot of fun for your guests.
Instruct a volunteer victim that you are going to press a

dime into his forehead, and he is to try to shake it loose without touching it.

The trick is that, after the dime has been firmly pressed to his forehead a few minutes before it is removed, it will still feel as if it is still there. The victim will shake his head frantically in attempting to get it off.

444. ONLY ONE WORD

Give two or three guests the following list of letters, with instructions to arrange them into only one word: D, N, W, E, O, N, O, R, O, Y, L. The trick is to arrange these letters so they spell "Only one word."

445. NEWSPAPER KEEPAWAY

Give two players a sheet of newspaper and challenge them both to stand on it at the same time without touching each other. The two may find this impossible until you spread the newspaper in a doorway with a guest on either side of the closed door.

446. EGG IN THE GLASS

Position a large drinking glass near the edge of a table. Place a tin pie pan on top of it and put a boiled egg in the pan so it is lying exactly over the top of the tumbler. Challenge guests to drop the egg into the glass without touching the egg, the pie pan, or the glass.

If no one is able to figure it out, show how it can be done.

When the arrangements were made, you carefully checked to see that the glass was placed over a leg of the table, and that the pan extended an inch or two beyond the edge of the table. Hold a broom beside the table leg, place your foot against it, and push against the leg. Pull the handle of the broom back and let it go with a snap, so that it will spring back, hitting against the edge of the pie pan. The pan will then go sailing across the room, and the egg will fall nicely into the glass.

447. FLOATING ARMS STUNT

Have guests take turns standing in a doorway narrow enough for the hands to press each side of the casing. Each person is told to keep his arms extended straight by his sides and press the outside of each hand hard against the door casing.

He must keep his arms stiff and continue pushing as hard as he can for from thirty seconds to a minute. Next, instruct him to step away from the doorway and let his arms relax at his side. They will automatically begin to rise.

448. MAGIC HAT

The magician holds three pieces of candy in one hand. He then chooses three hats worn by guests to the party. He elaborately questions these guests to assure the crowd that the hats have not in any way been prepared for the trick. The three pieces of candy are shown around so they can be identified. With a flourish, the magician eats all three.

He then asks, "Under which hat would you like to have those three pieces of candy be found?"

When someone points out one of the hats, the magician promptly places it on his head, saying, "All three pieces of candy are now under this hat."

449. BARNYARD HILARITY

Arrange for three confederates to be in on this stunt.

Place three chairs in a straight row. Bring in a victim and seat him between the two confederates. The third confederate acts as a director and very solemnly asks one of the confederates to take three steps toward him, then three backwards, bowing each step and imitating the sound made by the barnyard animal he names.

After three steps backward, he must turn to his chair and bow before sitting back down. After the first confederate has gone through this, the second repeats the ritual with a different animal noise. Then the victim is asked to do the same, imitating the cackle of a hen. While he is bowing and cackling, one of the seated confederates slips a hard boiled egg in his chair.

The egg is not discovered until the cackling "hen" turns and bows to his chair, before seating himself again.

450. FLIGHT TO THE MOON

Inform guests they are going to take a trip to the moon, but they must leave the room while the launch pad is prepared. Bring them back one at a time, and show each par-

ticipant a table leaf held by two strong accomplices. He is
then blindfolded and instructed to sit on the "space ship."

As he sits on the table leaf, he places one hand on each
pilot's head. The space capsule blasts off and rises into
space.

What actually happens, however, is that the two pilots
slowly lower themselves to the floor, keeping their backs
straight and heads held rigidly—until they are down on
their knees. The person sitting on the board will feel as
though he has been raised high into the air.

When this happens, instruct the passenger that the capsule has run into difficulty, and he must bail out. He will
probably refuse to jump. If he does, the two pilots dump
him out. He will feel quite sheepish when he learns the
floor is only a few inches away.

451. ENDLESS RAVELING

A good trick for a man to pull is to place a spool of
thread in his coat pocket, running one end through the coat
so that it hangs out a few inches. One of the other guests
will most likely be thoughtful enough to attempt to remove
the raveling and, to his surprise, discover that it seems to
have no end.

452. MEET THE DUKE AND DUTCHESS

Place two chairs at a distance apart that would allow a
third chair between. However, leave this space between
them empty. Instead, stretch a blanket tightly between the

two chairs so that when two people are seated on them it
appears there is a third chair in the center.

Bring guests into the room one at a time, instructing them
as they enter that they are going to be allowed the special
privilege of meeting the Duke and Dutchess, who sit in
grand style on the two outside chairs.

After a good deal of ceremony, tell the visitor he will be
permitted to sit between the Duke and Dutchess to have
his picture taken. When he is sitting down, the Duke and
Dutchess quickly rise, causing him to fall to the floor. It
might be a good idea to provide a soft landing with a few
pillows.

453. BARNYARD BEASTS

Inform your guests that each one will be assigned a farm
animal, whose sound he should imitate at a given signal.
Move around to each one, whispering in everyone's ear.
The funny trick is that you choose one guest to be the object of your prank. To him you whisper, "You imitate a
donkey." To everone else, however, you whisper, "Don't
make any sound." When the signal is given, the poor victim
chosen to be a donkey will find himself braying out a solo.

454. LOVE LETTER

Guests are seated in a circle with a leader designated to
begin a flowery love letter. He gives only the first word.
The next player in line supplies the second word. Continue
around the circle several times, until the love letter is fin-

ished—one word per guest at a time. This can prove to be quite comical.

You might want to assign a guest to keep a written record of the letter, as it progresses around the group and read it back when it is completed.

455. MEET MRS. LETTERFLY

Select a number of helpers and send the rest of the group out of the room. While they are gone, give a name ending in fly to each of the confederates. Some examples would be Miss Butterfly, Mr. Horsefly, Mrs. Dragonfly, Mr. Housefly, Miss Fruitfly, and Mrs. Letterfly.

Mrs. Letterfly is given a damp cloth to keep out of sight, as the guests are introduced.

When the first guest comes, tell him you would like to have him meet the fly family. Move down the line, introducing each member of the fly family until you come to the end and announce, "This is Mrs. Letterfly." The woman given this task does exactly that. She takes out her wet cloth and tosses it directly into the face of the astonished visitor.

456. DRY DOUSING

If you are gathered near a lake some night, give two men a large tub and ask them to go down to the water and fill it. Instead of water, however, they fill the tub with leaves and carry it back to the group as though it had become very heavy.

As they reach the guests, they suddenly raise the tub,

throwing its contents over the startled spectators, who expected to be drenched.

457. KEY RING STUNT

Hand one guest a key ring and tell him to try to poke his head through it. Insist it is possible to do this. If he fails to catch on, demonstrate the technique for him. Slip a finger through the ring, and then poke your head with it.

458. BLOW THE PENNY FROM THE DISH

Send all the guests into another room, and bring them back one at a time. As a guest returns, he is shown a dish with a penny in the center. He is then blindfolded and told to see if he can blow the penny off the dish.

While he is being blindfolded, two or three tablespoons of flour are placed on the dish so that when the unsuspecting guest gives a lusty blow, he is rewarded with a face full of flour.

459. MEET THE PHAROAH'S DAUGHTER

Players who are to be victims of this stunt are asked to leave the room. The others seat themselves in a semi-circle in front of the Pharoah's daughter, who occupies the throne with her left leg doubled under her. In its place is a carefully stuffed stocking put inside her shoe so that it resembles her own leg.

To better conceal this, have the royal lady dressed in long flowing robes made by draping a sheet carefully around her.

The first victim is summoned, and the leader explains in elaborate detail that in the court of the Pharoah's daughter there is an ancient custom—all who enter must shake the left leg of every person present in the room, reserving until last the honor of so greeting her highness.

The unwary victim commences to shake the left leg of players seated in a semi-circle around the throne, until he attempts to shake that of the Pharoah's daughter!

460. FASHION PARADE

Divide contestants into four or more groups and send each to a different room. The groups are supplied with a generous supply of newspapers and pins and are instructed to select one member to be the team's model.

The team members then proceed to concoct some type of paper costume for their model to wear. Bring all the groups back together again for a fashion parade.

Just for fun, you might dress some person in one of the new dresses actually made of paper and let her parade with the others.

461. HIDDEN CAMERA

Construct a large fake camera out of a cardboard box— the old fashioned kind with a large cloth draped around it. Be sure it has a good wide "lense" in front. The object of this stunt is that you place an actual camera inside the fake one. Arrange a humorous setting complete with lighting.

Ask for volunteers to pose as subjects in the stiff manner found in the old family albums. You might tape on mustaches, find a funny old bonnet—use any prop which will make the stunt more ridiculous.

Your guests should be convinced they are posing just for fun.

However, after a few "shots" have been taken, remove the real camera and show the subjects the "fun" was all yours, since you actually did take their pictures after all. These could be put on display at your next party.

462. OBSTACLE COURSE

Send players from the room, and permit them to return one at a time. As each player comes back, he is shown the living room floor which has been scattered with overturned chairs, boxes, waste basket, lamp, etc.

Then he is blindfolded and told he must attempt to make his way across the room without stumbling over any of the obstacles.

Announce in a loud voice that he should memorize these obstacles carefully so he will be able to avoid them. Continue the boistrous dialog, while he is being blindfolded and have someone remove all the obstacles but one. It will provide a good laugh for spectators to watch the blindfolded guest feel his way cautiously across the room, when there is only one obstacle in his way.

When he reaches the opposite side, remove his blindfold and show him how he has been fooled.

463. Mr. Crazy

Choose eleven guests and send them to separate areas, where they can work without observing one another. Give each guest a piece of paper cut a different size, a pencil, and scissors.

Tell each person he must draw one part of a man's anatomy. One draws the head, another is assigned the right eye, left eye, nose, mouth, torso, right arm, left arm, right leg, and left leg.

When finished, each one cuts out his own drawing and brings it to an assembly table where the crazy man is put together. He is certain to be quite an unusual looking fellow.

464. Penny and Glass Trick

Place three coins in a row on the tablecloth. Place three drinking glasses, upside down, on the table. Glasses partially cover the first and third coins, completely covering the center coin.

The trick is to remove the middle coin from under its glass without touching either the glass or the coin. To do this, merely scratch the tablecloth in front of the glass with a fingernail, scratching in a direction away from the glass and toward you. This technique will cause the middle coin to move in the direction of the finger.

465. No Spill

Challenge anyone to try turning a glass half-filled with

water upside down without spilling any of the contents. The trick is to place a piece of paper over the top of the glass and hold it flat while you quickly invert the glass. The paper will cling to the glass, and no water will spill out.

466. FIFTEEN COINS

Each two players have fifteen coins between them and alternate turns, taking one to three coins from the pile. The player forced to pick up the last coin loses the game.

The trick in winning is to pick up two coins, if you have first turn, or simply take the second draw.

467. TRICKY SPOON LIFT

Place the tip of a middle finger in the bowl of an ordinary teaspoon on the table. The trick is to attempt to pick up the spoon with the finger. To do this, rub that finger briskly on the tablecloth or on some clothing for a few seconds before pressing it against the spoon. This action will cause the spoon to adhere to the finger. The thumb should be used to balance the spoon.

468. BEND THE SPOON STUNT

A stunt to use at the table is to take an ordinary teaspoon and very carefully, with apparent effort, pretend to bend it.

This illusion is accomplished by slowly bringing the knuckles of the left hand and the right hand fingers together

until they touch. Then gradually reverse the process as the
spoon is "straightened."

A word of caution, though. Before anyone else is allowed
to try this stunt on good silver, be sure to explain what you
have done.

469. MUMMIFIED

Ask for three couples to volunteer for this stunt. Provide
each girl with a role of toilet paper and instruct her to make
an Egyptian mummy out of her partner. The couple first
finished with the job wins, provided not a bit of skin or
clothing is left showing.

470. SHAVE THE BALLOON

This is a good stunt for couples at a teen party.

Line up three or four couples at a time. The boy stands
with a toy balloon in his mouth. The girl covers the balloon with shaving cream and, at a given signal, attempts to
shave it all off with a razor blade.

It might be a good idea to drape a towel over the front
of each "customer," as he is certain to get a face full of
shaving cream when the balloon breaks.

PART TEN

.
.
.

STATION TO STATION

Whether the family is making a two hour jaunt to grand-mother's house, or driving all day on a vacation trip, hours spent in an automobile's cramped quarters may prove tedious both to the adults and children abroad.

When passing scenery is especially interesting, riders are likely to sit quietly. But during those long stretches, when the car begins to feel like a miniature prison on wheels, a few favorite traveling games may just save the day for driver and passengers alike.

The games included in this section utilize familiar objects seen along the highway. For some, you will need pencil and paper. For others, a keen eye is all that is necessary. Most of them will not only help pass the time, but may be of real educational value as well. Include a program of travel games on your vacation trip, and you may find the fun is in getting there.

471. HIGHWAY SCAVENGER HUNT

Prepare a list of twenty-five items for each player. Objects may be duplicated but make a different list for each person.

As they spot one of their listed items, players cross it off. They should point it out to the others in the car to be sure it counts.

Include some of the following: water tower, blue silo, man on a tractor, black horse, pink house, flag flying, green sign, etc. Of course you may have to adapt the lists to climate conditions, as well to the type of country through which you are passing.

Award a special prize to the player first to complete his list.

472. AUTOMOBILE TWENTY-ONE

This is a game to keep riders busy for miles on end.

Players can work together, or individually. They are to look for license plates containing numbers from 1 to 21.

Only one numeral may be taken from one license plate, and players can not count a 9, for example, until they have seen 1 through 8. You can have the players take turns watching license plates on approaching cars.

Number one through twenty-one need not appear in the correct order on a license, but both must be on the same plate. That is, a license number could be 04619 and still count as 10.

473. Color Race

Prepare a slip of paper, one for each player, and write a common auto paint color on each. If there are four players, for example, the slips might list white, blue, red, and green. Shuffle them up and have each player draw one.

Players then begin to keep a tally of the number of cars they can spot in the color they have drawn. You might want to restrict this to moving vehicles only. The first player to count 50 (or 100, if traffic is heavy) wins.

474. Unusual License Plates

See how long it takes your travelers to find the following license plates:

1. A license plate with any three numbers or letters in a row.
2. A plate with the outline of the state issuing it.
3. A license with letters only.
4. The license plate of an official government car.
5. A license plate containing letters that spell a person's name.
6. A license plate from a state on either coast.
7. A license plate with three or less letters and numbers.
8. A license from outside your country.

475. I Saw It First

A lot of fun can be had on the road by awarding points for different items seen along the way. This can be limited to just one subject, such as white horses—or points can be awarded for different types of buildings, signs, etc.

One person acts as the scorekeeper and records the points for all players. Some travelers play the game by limiting one side of the road to one group of players with the remaining players watching the other side. In this way, a team counts only those items on their side of the road.

476. CARELESS DRIVERS

A good object lesson can be learned by having your riders keep a list of the careless drivers they see on a trip. Even young children soon learn to spot a reckless maneuver, a speeding car, littering the road, etc.

Such a travel pastime will be a valuable aid in educating future drivers.

477. INTERSECTION SONG SWITCH

If you enjoy singing together on the road, this is a good idea to try. One person leads the group in a number of well-known choruses or hymns. When an intersection is passed, however, no matter where you are in the song, immediately switch to another tune. If you travel on a long stretch without coming to any intersection, you repeat the same chorus or hymn.

478. THE NAME'S THE THING

Players write out the letters of their full name down the

side of a sheet of paper. As the game begins, each person writes the name of an item spotted along the road that begins with a letter in his name.

An item may only be used once on the list. Thus Mary might complete her first name by sighting a mule, an auditorium, a rock, and a yard .

479. THAT ONE IS DIFFERENT

Keep a list of the different cars seen on the trip. To be counted, an automobile must be different in some manner from any other. Watch for different colors and styles—and such things as a luggage rack or sticker display.

480. ONE HUNDRED POINTS

Players take turns reading off license numbers on approaching cars. Total the first and last digit on the plate and award a small prize to the player first to reach one hundred.

481. AUTO MAKES AND MODELS

As you travel down the highway, maintain a list of the makes and models of the automobiles you meet. On a super highway with one way traffic, this could be done by counting both the cars you pass and those that pass you. This can prove to be interesting and educational both to the children and the adults.

482. Billboard Alphabet

Divide the travelers into teams, with one group watching all billboards on the left side of the road and the other team watching those on the right. As the signs appear, each player scans the message for letters of the alphabet.

These must be located only in the order they appear in the alphabet. Thus, when a player has spotted an A, he begins looking for a B, etc. Only one letter may be taken from each sign.

483. Seen Along the Way

Before leaving on the trip, make a list of special objects which might possibly be seen from the car. These might include a haystack, historical marker, a rider on horseback, a new house being built, etc. Then, as you travel, award points to the first passenger spotting each of these objects.

484. How Far Is That Water Tower

Everyone in the car has a chance to play this game. The driver looks ahead down the road and asks riders to guess how far away an object is. Distance is then accurately measured on the speedometer.

485. Adding

This is a game for older players. The leader points out a

car and riders must quickly total up the numbers on its license plate. If the plate read VL 621935, the total would be 26. The object, of course, is to see who can first total the numbers most correctly.

486. Sound Effects

One player is chosen to be "it" and starts the game by spotting passing objects with sounds that can be imitated. If he sees a pig, he makes a grunting sound, tweets for a bird, whistles for a train, etc.

The first player to spot the object being imitated gets one point.

After ten imitations, another player becomes "it." Continue playing until everyone has had a turn being "it," then total up the points.

487. Alphabet Objects

Riders look for an object beginning with the letter A, then B, C and so on through the alphabet. You may decide to omit the letters X and Z. The first player calling out an object as it is passed may count it while others must spot another.

488. Bible Subjects

Have individual contestants or team members see who can discover the most objects along the way which are in some way related to objects in the Bible. A mule, children, a stream, large rock, cattle, and sheep are all possibilities.

489. Ten Pairs

Each player picks a digit to look for on license plates. One may hunt for an 8, another a 3, etc. When a player spots a pair of the number he has chosen, he scores one point. The player first to find ten pairs wins.

490. Fifty Mile Rotate

If your automobile is small and there are several passengers, try this little game to avoid quarrels over choice seating positions. Every fifty miles, the driver calls out, "Rotate." Riders then move to the right one place, with the traveler sitting by the right side back window, scooting to the front seat. This might also be done by taking a brief rest stop along the road, thus giving the driver a chance to stretch.

491. Blink

Here is a new travel game that will help keep the younger tourists pleasantly occupied for many miles. It will probably work best in an automobile, but you might try it while riding in a train or bus as well.

Players decide on a visible distant object, such as a schoolhouse, gas station, or signboard. Then everyone covers his eyes until he thinks they are passing the object. He quickly opens his eyes and calls, "Blink." In this way, individual players make decisions on the distance traveled.

If traffic is light, the driver can add to the fun by slowing down or speeding up just a bit to confuse the guessers.

492. BOOKS OF THE BIBLE

As you travel down the road, see how long it takes to name all the books of the Bible in correct order by watching for the first letter of each to appear on passing license plates. You must locate a plate with a G for Genesis, one with an E for Exodus, etc. This is a fun game to play as a group contest.

493. CHARACTERS OF THE BIBLE

Make a list of Bible characters for each player and have them watch for license plates which contain the first letter of each. Or you might spot a license with several letters and award points to each contestant first to name a Bible character whose name begins with a letter in the plate.

494. ANIMALS ALONG THE ROAD

While riding in the car, one player or team watches one side of the road, with another player or group watching the other. Count one point for each cow or horse spotted, two points for every pig, dog or cat, five points for every goose, and ten points for a white horse.

If a herd of animals is passed, count only ten points for those animals. Each time a cemetery is passed, deduct ten points from the score. The player or team first to reach one hundred wins.

495. Jalopies

Keep a running count of the number of vintage automobiles seen along the road. Set a limit on the year or make, and then have one person familiar with car models serve as referee.

496. Good Enough To Eat

Assign one side of the road for one team and the other for the opposite team. Then work out a system in which you count one point for every billboard advertizing an edible product.

497. First Initials

Another traveling pastime is to award points everytime someone spots an object which begins with the first letter of his name. Susan would earn points when a silo or stream was spotted. Timothy would keep a sharp eye on the landscape for trains, towers, etc.

498. Parts Of Our Car

Start the game by having one player think of a part of the car and give only the first letter of the word. For example, if he thinks of windshield, he announces the letter w. Each player in turn is allowed three guesses.

The one who guesses picks the next part. If nobody is able to guess, a player has another turn choosing a part.

499. Touring Storytellers

When the passing scenery is drab, or you are traveling after dark, try this new adaptation of the chain story. One person begins telling a colorful tale and continues until the speedometer has recorded exactly one mile. At that point, someone appointed to keep check calls out, "Stop."

The story must be picked up by the next player, who carries the narrative during the next one mile limit. If you have only a few riders, this can be repeated two or three times until the person who started the story brings it to a logical conclusion .

500. How Far Have We Traveled?

Have each player close his eyes as he attempts to correctly guess when one mile has been traveled. This will be fun, as some riders will be positive a mile has passed only to learn that the car has gone perhaps half a mile. Others will keep their eyes closed too long.

Caution players that when they do open their eyes, they

must be quiet about the speedometer listing, so they will not give away any clues to the others as to whether or not they should open their eyes.

501. TIME FLIES

The above game can be played on the basis of time passed. Have someone hold a watch and keep track of five minutes. During that period, everyone tries to estimate how many miles to the tenth the car has traveled.

502. STORES

When you are passing through an urban area, divide the players into teams, giving one side of the street to each team. Teams earn one point by spotting a grocery store, two points for a shoe store, three points for a drug store, four points for a barber shop, etc.